WHO
DO YOU THINK
YOU ARE?

THE ESSENTIAL GUIDE TO
TRACING YOUR FAMILY HISTORY

MEGAN SMOLENYAK²

PENGUIN BOOKS

PENGUIN BOOKS
Published by the Penguin Group
Penguin Group (USA) Inc., 375 Hudson Street, New York, New York 10014, U.S.A.
Penguin Group (Canada), 90 Eglinton Avenue East, Suite 700, Toronto,
Ontario, Canada M4P 2Y3 (a division of Pearson Penguin Canada Inc.)
Penguin Books Ltd, 80 Strand, London WC2R 0RL, England
Penguin Ireland, 25 St Stephen's Green, Dublin 2, Ireland (a division of Penguin Books Ltd)
Penguin Group (Australia), 250 Camberwell Road, Camberwell,
Victoria 3124, Australia (a division of Pearson Australia Group Pty Ltd)
Penguin Books India Pvt Ltd, 11 Community Centre,
Panchsheel Park, New Delhi – 110 017, India
Penguin Group (NZ), 67 Apollo Drive, Rosedale, North Shore 0632,
New Zealand (a division of Pearson New Zealand Ltd)
Penguin Books (South Africa) (Pty) Ltd, 24 Sturdee Avenue,
Rosebank, Johannesburg 2196, South Africa

Penguin Books Ltd, Registered Offices:
80 Strand, London WC2R 0RL, England

First published in the United States of America by Viking Penguin,
a member of Penguin Group (USA) Inc. 2009
Published in Penguin Books 2010

1   3   5   7   9   10   8   6   4   2

Pages 203–204 constitute an extension of this copyright page.

THE LIBRARY OF CONGRESS HAS CATALOGED THE HARDCOVER EDITION AS FOLLOWS:
Smolenyak, Megan.
Who do you think you are? : the essential guide to tracing
your family history / Wall to Wall Media and Megan Smolenyak.
p.   cm.
ISBN 978-0-670-02163-5 (hc.)
ISBN 978-0-14-311891-6 (pbk.)
1. Genealogy.   I. Wall to Wall Media.   II. Title.
CS16.S646 2010
929'.1072—dc22   2009038744

Printed in the United States of America

To Col. George C. Smolenyak,
for the unique name that sparked
my interest in genealogy
and so much more

Contents

Introduction

Yes, it's true that there are people who think family history is boring, whose eyes glaze over at the very mention of the g-word—genealogy. But they couldn't be more wrong, and the fact that you're holding this book shows that you're one of the 79 percent of Americans who have figured that out.

The truth is that genealogy is absolutely addicting. Ask anyone who's been at it for even a little while and you'll inevitably hear tales of surfing the Internet in pajamas at three in the morning, climbing over fences to get to abandoned cemeteries, and purposely trying to get locked into libraries overnight. Once you get started, you won't want to stop.

Why? The thrill of the hunt. Genealogy is your own personal history mystery. You get to play detective, chasing scattered clues across the centuries. It's time travel at its very best, and in a way, it's all about you. As you learn about your ancestors, you'll likely discover why you're so musical or such a globe trekker. Our roots claim us in ways we don't even realize.

And the good news is that there's no such thing as a boring family. Once you embark on your quest, there's no telling what you might find. A great-aunt who was a con woman, a third great-grandfather who was a Civil War hero, an immigrant great-grandfather who came to

America to escape the law, or maybe an ancestor who invented the toilet (in which case, my family thanks yours).

Sure, you'll take a few wrong turns along the way, but that's half the fun. Who wants to read a mystery novel where you can figure out the ending by page 11? With family history, there's always another clue or ancestor to pursue, and this book is here to serve as your guide.

There's a good chance that this book caught your eye because you've watched a few episodes of *Who Do You Think You Are?* and are feeling inspired to do a little sleuthing of your own, but people feel the genealogical tug for a host of reasons. In my case, it was a sixth-grade homework assignment that got me started. I was instructed to go home one night and ask my parents where my surname came from. Slightly misinformed (as I would learn a few years later), I was told that the Smolenyaks were Russians from Smolensk. It seemed to make sense, so the next day when we put our names up on a world map in our countries of origin, I claimed the whole of the then–Soviet Union for myself. I still remember feeling sorry for all my classmates crowded around the British Isles. That was the first time I realized there was something a little different about my heritage, so I quickly morphed into the twisted kid who saved her allowance not to buy the latest hit song, but to purchase another death certificate. While my classmates were counting the days to their sixteenth birthdays so they could get a driver's license, I anticipated that day because I would finally be old enough to go to the National Archives. I am, in short, one of the more obsessed genealogical geeks out there, and I like to think that qualifies me on some level to be your usher into this retro-world.

Before we jump in, I'd like to make one more comment about the g-word. I'm as avid a genealogist as you'll find, but many find the word intimidating, confusing, or both. And it gets a bit tiresome being mistaken for a gynecologist or geologist (one of my neighbors still asks me about coal mines because I haven't had the courage to correct her understanding of what I do). Because of that, I'll use the words *genealogy* and *genealogist* throughout this book, but I'll also toss in terms like *family historian* and *genie*. "Genie" is not a word commonly used in this field. In fact, some of my fellow professionals will likely bristle at it, but I sprinkle my conversation with "genie" not to be disrespectful, but with affection. Genealogy has an amazing ability to reconnect families separated by centuries and oceans, and I believe that there's genuinely something a little magical about that. So I hope that you'll accept "genie" as it's intended, as a friendly and fitting diminutive. With that said, let's dive in.

WHO DO YOU THINK YOU ARE?

1

PREPARING FOR YOUR
ANCESTOR HUNT

As with so many activities, a little preparation can go a long way. After watching an episode of *Who Do You Think You Are?*, it's understandable that you might feel a sudden urge to peek into your family's past. For many, the first instinct is to jump on the computer, but if you can discipline yourself to do a little offline sleuthing beforehand, you'll ultimately go a lot farther a lot faster.

Investigate the clues you've probably got tucked away in your attic, closets, and basement and call your older relatives (think of them as witnesses to your family history), and you'll avoid getting stumped or derailed early on. This chapter will offer ideas and strategies to help you get off to a solid start, as well as dodge common pitfalls.

WHERE DO YOU WANT TO GO?

A useful starting point is to ask yourself what you hope to accomplish. Do you want to learn more about the origins of your surname or everything you can about your family tree? Is your goal to identify all eight of your great-grandparents, all sixteen great-great-grandparents, or as many ancestors as you can possibly uncover? Are you aiming to identify your ancestral hometown in Italy so you can visit during the vacation you've planned next year, or perhaps any military forefathers to find out more about your family's service to our country (yes, fore*mothers* may have served as well, but historically speaking, it's mostly males)? Maybe you're tackling a school assignment about Ellis Island or helping one of your kids with a family history-oriented project—or perhaps you're gathering up what you can in time to put together a keepsake album for your parents' golden wedding anniversary. There are countless reasons to play with genealogy, and it helps to spend even a few minutes up front to think about what your objectives are. While we all start off the same way, those interested in Ellis Island arrivals will ultimately tap into different resources from those intrigued by their family's participation in the Civil War.

Of course, it's perfectly acceptable to jump in to see what you might discover. Many are simply curious about the entertaining stories that might be found dangling from the branches of their family tree. It used to be that royal roots gave you bragging rights, but these days, rebels, rogues, and renegades earn you about the same amount of genealogical capital. I'd say that the exchange rate is roughly one king to one outlaw, and discovering either in your past will likely whet your appetite for history. Finding an ancestor who missed the *Titanic* because of illness or helped build the Erie Canal will suddenly produce an insatiable thirst for knowledge about topics that seemed beyond tedious in your high school history textbooks. That direct link—knowing that someone who contributed to your DNA was there—changes everything, so don't be alarmed to find yourself making field trips, searching for out-of-print books, or even becoming that annoying know-it-all you used to roll your eyes at.

How long will all this take? That's up to you. If you've decided to transcribe the tombstones in a neglected cemetery for your Eagle Scout project, there's a fairly apparent ending point, but if you want to find out everything you possibly can about your heritage, that's a different story. There's always another ancestor to research if you feel like it, and many enjoy the thrill of the hunt so much that they never want it to end. Regardless of what you initially set out to accomplish, it's a good idea to prepare yourself for the slippery slope phenomenon. Even if you tell yourself you're just putting together a chart for the upcoming reunion, you might find yourself still adding to it years after the event. But if that happens, it will be because you're having too much fun to stop.

START WITH WHAT YOU KNOW

I don't blame you if the thought running through your head at the moment is, "Well, duh!" It probably sounds mind-blowingly obvious to suggest that you start with what you know, but you'd be surprised how many people don't.

I think it's fair to say that we are a nation of impatient people. With so many opportunities for instant gratification, we've become accustomed to fast results and expect our roots served up the same way. So it's only natural that most of us embarking on a genealogical quest will impulsively grab a laptop and do a vanity search. Google your name and—poof!—instant roots, right? Another favorite point of entry is that famous ancestor you've heard mention of. Your name is Boone, so you must be related to Daniel Boone. Find his family tree online, and all you have to do is locate yourself in one of the branches. Centuries of family history will unfold before you in minutes.

You might think I'm exaggerating, but any librarian can regale you with tales of patrons who called wanting to pick up their family history at the reference desk or even the drive-through window (no kidding). If you're venturing into the world of genealogy now, you'll be pleased to hear that you were smart to wait. While I'm glad to have started in the old-school, paper-and-pencil, snail-mail days, you will definitely be able to find out much more about your family considerably faster than I did. What took me months might take you a couple of hours, but we're not quite at the just-add-water stage.

The danger of jumping in with no preparation is the risk of, well, barking up the wrong tree. It is astonishingly easy to assume your way into someone else's family tree (say, by confusing two people who happened to have the same name), only to discover some time later that you have no connection whatsoever to that family. Or perhaps you'll correctly latch yourself on to someone else's pedigree—after all, that was definitely your grandmother in there—only to learn later that the tree is riddled with errors elsewhere.

The tree you found online may be based on a century-old book found in the finest libraries, but these weighty tomes don't come with warning labels that many doing genealogy (or having it done for them) in the old days were doing so to prove illustrious roots, and there were Victorian rip-off artists only too happy to provide them. Want to wind up a hard-core genealogist? Just mention the name Gustav Anjou and watch the reaction. Genealogies he dreamed up before you existed continue to fool people and pollute family trees today, and there are more victims of this ancestral mischief out there than you'd think. Bouncing around the country on book and speaking tours, I've sporadically encountered folks who have assured me they don't need any help because they already have their roots traced back to Adam and Eve. I don't have the heart to burst their bubble, but I'll say this much. If you, as I have, find a tree online that starts with Adam and Eve and shows one of their children being born in British Columbia, Canada, a little skepticism wouldn't be out of order.

GO ON A TREASURE HUNT

Let's say you've taken a few minutes to jot down what you know about your family—maybe some names, dates, and places pertaining to you and your parents, and even a couple of your grandparents. What next?

Now's a good time to rediscover your own home. Most of us are

clueless about all the treasures and tidbits lurking in our closets, draw-
ers, basements, and attics. Many a genealogist has been chagrined to
finally determine an elusive ancestor's name after a year of research,
only to find this same information in a suitcase of papers tucked into
the corner of their own cellar. One of the best possible hauls? A stash of
old letters—bonus points if they still have their envelopes with precious
names and addresses. Other items to keep your eyes open for include:

- Birth, marriage, and death certificates
- Newspaper clippings, including obituaries and wedding
  and anniversary announcements
- Naturalization and citizenship papers, including pass-
  ports and visas
- Religious records (e.g., baptismal, bar mitzvah, etc.)
- Family Bible
- Letters (and addressed envelopes)
- Diaries and journals
- Photo albums (especially photos with the name of the pho-
  tography studio imprinted or details written on back)
- Heirlooms such as engraved items, samplers, and quilts
- Any other documents pertaining to your ancestors (e.g.,
  military, school, occupational, business, land, legal, etc.)

Genealogy guru Loretto Szucs offers even more ideas in "Lou's 300
Family History Sources Checklist" (go to AncestryMagazine.com, enter
"Lou's 300" in the search field, and click on "Home Sources"). After you're
done poking through your own hiding places, you might want to see if
Mom is willing to let you have a look at hers. (Hint: When scavenging for
pieces of your family's past, play the odds by starting with the women; we
tend to be the hoarders or protectors, depending on your perspective.) She
could refuse, but it's more likely that she'll be happy to hear of your sudden interest and let you explore a few trunks or boxes in the attic.

LIVING LIBRARIES

Once you're done looking through Mom's attic, you might want to sit down and talk with her. For that matter, if you have any relatives even twenty minutes older than you, stop reading right now and pick up the phone! These people are living libraries. What they can tell you off the top of their heads can shave months off your research time.

When it comes to older relatives, less is sometimes more. It's often more fruitful to conduct several mini-interviews rather than one intensive one. Of course, if you're traveling to speak with them, you might not have that luxury, but if they live nearby, consider a series of brief talks, as opposed to a marathon session.

You'll want to give some thought to your questions in advance. There are plenty of resources to help you develop a list of likely topics (you'll find some in the appendix), and the more specific you can be, the better. In fact, it sometimes helps to think of a couple of different ways to broach the same subject. Older relatives often take the information that lives in their brains for granted and have a tendency to assume you already know what they know. Out of consideration, they'll try to avoid "boring" you, so you can easily wind up missing all sorts of genealogical gems.

I recall my last interview with my great-aunt Verna. I had spoken with her about the family several times before, and she always protested that she didn't know much because she was the youngest. But this time she made a random comment that her aunt Gabriella had red hair. Verna was born in Pennsylvania, but her aunt was born in Europe, and until that moment, I never knew that Gabriella had come to America. I had asked Verna directly about any siblings her immigrant parents had, but she only mentioned a couple of her mother's. It turned out that she hadn't bothered to tell me about her father's sister because they didn't stay in touch. I don't remember the question that provoked the red-hair response, but if I hadn't somehow revisited the topic, I'd probably never have found the second cousin who eventually accompanied me on a trip back to our native village in Slovakia.

It's also a good idea to ask about anyone else your older relatives think you should contact. Canvassing your relatives in this manner will turn up countless details that may not have trickled down your direct line. I once had the good fortune of chain-calling my way to a distant cousin whose immigrant grandmother was the sister of my immigrant great-great-grandmother—in other words, he was two generations closer to the old country than I was. He didn't know how to spell it, but told me phonetically the name of the town his grandmother came from and I was able to find it on a map of Ireland. The next year, I had the pleasure of visiting the church and cemetery of our shared ancestors in the auld sod.

Finally, you've probably already thought of this, but as long as your relatives are comfortable with your doing so, record your interviews. Video is ideal, but if they're the type who squirms when a camera's present, they're probably not going to open up to you. Audio is less obtrusive, and a useful option for these situations. Recording your talk will free you up to truly listen, ask better questions, and follow up on unexpected nuggets that emerge. I regret to this day that I wasn't better equipped when interviewing an elderly cousin who made matter-of-fact remarks about my great-grandfather killing his wife, my great-grandmother. This was news to me. I had decided to speak with this far-flung cousin only because she was the last in my U.S.-based family born in Ukraine.

The flip side is that I fortunately did tape-record a conversation with my nana when she was ninety years old. As we often do, I somehow expected her to live forever, but she passed away three months later. As we chatted, I urged her to tell me the family stories I had heard so many times growing up that they almost bored me—you know, the ones that make everyone groan? When I finally mustered the nerve to listen to the tape (it can take a while after losing a loved one), I was stunned by how much my mind had already managed to jumble. I thought I knew these stories by heart, but I already had some of the details wrong—and I was the family historian.

CHART YOUR WAY

About the time you're wrapping up your treasure hunt and that first talk with your mother, you're probably going to find yourself looking for a way to organize all the information you're gathering. The easiest way to do this is to create a chart that's often referred to as a family tree. Fortunately, you have plenty of options for doing this. While I started back in the Dark Ages with paper, I strongly recommend that you take advantage of software and online tree services for doing this (see the appendix for popular alternatives). They make it easy to modify your entries over time, print out useful reports, and keep track of all the relationships (trust me, you don't want to try to keep third cousins twice removed straight in your head—and incidentally, we'll explain "*nth* cousins *x* times removed" in chapter 7, "The Best of the Rest").

A family tree, also referred to as a pedigree (yes, as with show dogs and racehorses), is a handy way for organizing the most basic of genealogical information—names, dates, and places. While just about any event in a person's life can be recorded, genies tend to focus initially on births, marriages, and deaths. These milestones are the fundamental building blocks of family trees.

Start by entering your own details—your full name at birth, as well as the date and place of your birth, and then your marriage date and place. Incidentally, all women are listed by their maiden names, partly because you'll need that information to find records pertaining to them before they married as you work your way back through the generations. Once you're done with yourself, repeat this process for your parents. If you're doing a family tree for your children, you can start with them and add yourself and your spouse as their parents.

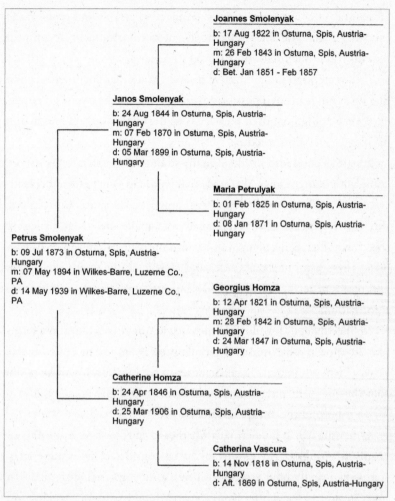

Joannes Smolenyak

b: 17 Aug 1822 in Osturna, Spis, Austria-Hungary
m: 26 Feb 1843 in Osturna, Spis, Austria-Hungary
d: Bet. Jan 1851 - Feb 1857

Janos Smolenyak

b: 24 Aug 1844 in Osturna, Spis, Austria-Hungary
m: 07 Feb 1870 in Osturna, Spis, Austria-Hungary
d: 05 Mar 1899 in Osturna, Spis, Austria-Hungary

Maria Petrulyak

b: 01 Feb 1825 in Osturna, Spis, Austria-Hungary
d: 08 Jan 1871 in Osturna, Spis, Austria-Hungary

Petrus Smolenyak

b: 09 Jul 1873 in Osturna, Spis, Austria-Hungary
m: 07 May 1894 in Wilkes-Barre, Luzerne Co., PA
d: 14 May 1939 in Wilkes-Barre, Luzerne Co., PA

Georgius Homza

b: 12 Apr 1821 in Osturna, Spis, Austria-Hungary
m: 28 Feb 1842 in Osturna, Spis, Austria-Hungary
d: 24 Mar 1847 in Osturna, Spis, Austria-Hungary

Catherine Homza

b: 24 Apr 1846 in Osturna, Spis, Austria-Hungary
d: 25 Mar 1906 in Osturna, Spis, Austria-Hungary

Catherina Vascura

b: 14 Nov 1818 in Osturna, Spis, Austria-Hungary
d: Aft. 1869 in Osturna, Spis, Austria-Hungary

A portion of my family tree showing ancestors' names along with birth, marriage, and death dates and places. *(courtesy of the author)*

Many are also able to record bits and pieces for their grandparents, but it's not at all unusual to get stumped on Grandma's maiden name. If this happens to you, don't worry. Just enter what you know for now. If you're estimating (say, you recall your grandfather passing away in the 1970s, but don't remember when), enter the information, but use the built-in flexibility provided. Try a date range (1970–1979) or put "abt" (about) or "circa" in front of the date. Later when you find proof of the exact date, you'll be able to update it, but in the meantime, it can help remind you of the rough time period to research.

If the certificates, diplomas, obituaries, and other documents you've dug up at home make it possible to go back farther than your grandparents, keep going. Standard practice is to start with yourself and march back one generation at a time.

It's also a good idea to add as many siblings as you can to get a more complete picture. Down the road, this will help your research considerably and make it easier to fit in the assorted cousins you'll find along the way. If you do this, you'll be able to make use of family group sheets, another convenient way of summarizing what you've discovered. These list a husband, wife, and children, along with their dates and places of birth, marriage, and death, spouses, and sources for this information.

While you can download family tree and family group sheet forms (see the appendix for links), all genealogy software and most online tree services will automatically generate them for you. Both will help you spot the gaps—missing ancestors or events—and give you a road map for your beyond-the-family research.

One issue worth pondering is whether to start (or later upload) your family tree online. There's privacy to be considered, but online environments usually offer a menu of privacy settings, including one that makes your tree available only to you and those you invite. And in most instances, you can control whether those you invite are able to view the tree, contribute to it, or make changes.

Of course, one of the main reasons for putting your tree on the Internet is the opportunity to collaborate with others. Maybe your aunt will dig out some photos after your interview, scan them and attach them to your shared tree. It's funny how snippets of a family's history drift down different branches, and having a centralized tree online can be an efficient way of reassembling the photos that went to your cousin Kathy and the military discharge papers that went to your cousin David. It's

Family Group Sheet

Husband: Janko Petrulyak

Born: Abt. 1782	in: Ostuma, Spis, Austria-Hungary
Married: 25 Feb 1815	in: Ostuma, Spis, Austria-Hungary
Died: 12 Jan 1853	in: Ostuma, Spis, Austria-Hungary
Father: Petrus Petrulyak	
Mother: Maria Smolenyak	
Other Spouses: Anna Pavlicsak	

Wife: Anna Szkibiak

Born: Abt. 1786	in: Ostuma, Spis, Austria-Hungary
Died: 05 Mar 1830	in: Ostuma, Spis, Austria-Hungary

CHILDREN

1 M
Name: Joannes Petrulyak
Born: 08 Oct 1815 in: Ostuma, Spis, Austria-Hungary; sponsors: Janko Kusnyirak & Anna Szmolenyak
Married: 01 Mar 1840 in: Ostuma, Spis, Austria-Hungary; witnesses: Joannes Figlyar & Joannes Szmolenyak
Spouse: Maria Kusnyirak

2 M
Name: Michael Petrulyak
Born: 25 Sep 1821 in: Ostuma, Spis, Austria-Hungary
Married: 15 Nov 1841 in: Ostuma, Spis, Austria-Hungary
Spouse: Maria Solitz

3 F
Name: Maria Petrulyak
Born: 01 Feb 1825 in: Ostuma, Spis, Austria-Hungary
Died: 08 Jan 1871 in: Ostuma, Spis, Austria-Hungary
Married: 26 Feb 1843 in: Ostuma, Spis, Austria-Hungary
Spouse: Joannes Smolenyak
Married: 09 Feb 1857 in: Ostuma, Spis, Austria-Hungary
Spouse: Joannes Figlyar
Married: 21 Feb 1859 in: Ostuma, Spis, Austria-Hungary
Spouse: Joannes Illyczak

Part of a family group sheet shows all the details for a nuclear family—and yes, daughter Maria was the marrying kind. *(courtesy of the author)*

also likely that popping your tree online will eventually attract some distant cousins you've never heard of (even those overseas), and you never know which pieces of your shared puzzle they might have.

Another factor is cost. Online tree services tend to operate as social networks, meaning the tree is free, but you'll probably be subjected to advertising. Others offer the tree portion free, but charge to access and attach records pertaining to your family. These can range up to three hundred dollars a year, but that can be quite reasonable when shared across several of the family members belonging to the same tree. It can also be very cost-effective compared to making trips to repositories to find the same records that reside online, but the choice is yours.

One last feature you'll want to look for in making your decision is GEDCOM functionality. GEDCOM is essentially a common language that allows data entered in one family history software program or online environment to be pulled into another. To allow yourself future flexibility, you'll want to be sure that yours lets you save your data this way so you won't have to start over if you decide to shift platforms. Make sure that your online service permits you to save your tree as a file that can be understood by any genealogical software package or vice versa.

DON'T BELIEVE EVERYTHING YOU READ OR HEAR

We know this in everyday life, but for some reason, we seem to ignore this counsel when it comes to genealogy. Passed down to us as precious cargo by our parents and other elders, our family lore takes on the veneer of inviolate truth. But no matter how sincere the intentions of the messenger, chances are that more than a little distortion has crept in.

Just think of the game "telephone" you played as a kid. You whispered, "Did the ice cream melt?" into the ear of your playmate, she passed it on to the next child, and it emerged five whispers later as, "Did the mice scream 'help'?" This is what happens to family tales. Through a combination of misunderstanding, forgetfulness, embellishment, and deliberate twisting, they morph over the generations. There's virtually always a seed of truth embedded, but accepting the entire story as fact will often throw off your research.

Blinded by the tale, we get locked into a paradigm that prevents us from finding the reality. For example, many people are convinced that Grandpa came through Ellis Island only to learn—when someone else dared to question the legend—that he immigrated through Baltimore or by train from Canada.

One of the most startling examples of this is Annie Moore, the first immigrant to arrive at Ellis Island. Statues of her stand both there and at the Cobh Heritage Centre in Ireland, but that didn't stop us from getting her story wrong. For years, people believed a saga that had her moving to Texas and eventually New Mexico before meeting a tragic end. While working on a documentary, I discovered that this adventurous Annie wasn't the one who arrived at Ellis Island from Ireland.

I blogged a contest to uncover the real Annie, and six weeks later, we learned the truth. She never left New York City and her actual story was typical of the hardscrabble existence of many immigrants. Annie died in 1924—yesterday in genealogical terms—and yet, we all fell for a romantic myth. Why? Because an elderly woman announced to her family that her mother—another Annie Moore—was *the* Annie Moore, and no one ever questioned the claim. That was all it took for a touch of wishful thinking to slip into American history.

And don't think just because it's in black and white that it's necessarily accurate. This is particularly true of immigrant ancestors who often didn't know their own birth dates. For instance, you should routinely question the names given for an immigrant's parents on his or her death certificate because the informant was probably a child of the immigrant who never even met his old-country grandparents. Confusion can creep in in other ways as well. When my grandfather's birth certificate listed Greece as the birthplace of his mother, I squandered valuable time seeking my Greek great-grandmother, only to discover she emigrated from Poland. How could Greece and Poland be muddled? She was of the Greek Catholic faith.

Returning to Annie Moore (and we'll hear still more about her later), finding her birth records in Ireland proved difficult because of the existing paper trail. Passenger records listed her as either thirteen or fifteen, and newspapers of the day made a fuss about the "fact" that she had arrived on her fifteenth birthday on January 1, 1892. So when researchers first looked for her records, they focused on 1877, but students in Cork planning to make a film about Annie's life were a little less literal and found her birth records several years earlier. Even in her teens, Annie was already fibbing about her age.

This doesn't mean you need to toss aside the family stories and discount everything you find, but it does mean you should examine every piece of data with a critical eye. To give you a head start, here's a short list of commonly held beliefs that should make you wary:

- *Our name was changed at Ellis Island.* No, it wasn't. Your ancestor changed it after the fact, probably Americanizing it by lopping off a couple of syllables (Villapiano becomes Villa), translating (Weiss becomes White), dropping accents or "extra" letters (Smolenyak used to begin with Szm), picking an Anglo-sounding version (Lewinsky becomes Lewis), and so forth. Ellis Island was staffed with people who spoke dozens of languages and were mostly checking names against lists generated at the port of departure. In spite of what you might have seen in *The Godfather*, they didn't substitute village names for surnames or arbitrarily assign "more American" names to immigrants.

- *We're descended from a Cherokee princess.* Not so much. I'm not sure why, but with this tale, it's always Cherokee and it's always a princess. No one ever claims to have a Chippewa Cree prince for an ancestor. White settlers sometimes referred to the daughter of a chief or other Native woman of some note as a princess, but there's no such thing as an Indian princess. What *might* be true is that you have some Native ancestry, but that claim should also be investigated, even if you have a photo of an ancestor who's described as having "olive skin with high cheek bones."

- *Three brothers came to America. One went north, one went south, and one went west.* You can cut yourself a little more slack on this one because there obviously must be some families where this is true, though the more typical pattern was for whole families to come as a unit or chain migration—meaning the father or maybe one brother came first, made enough money to send back for another brother or two to join him, who then made enough money to send for still more family members. More often than not, the north-south-west aspect is an attempt to link geographically dispersed families of the same surname. Fortunately, with DNA, it's now possible to test such theories (more on this later), but if this assertion pops up in your family, exercise a little caution.

- *Here's your coat of arms!* This isn't so much a myth as a marketing phenomenon. If you've ever seen those carts in malls that purport to give you a history of your family name along with your coat of arms, please don't be fooled. Heraldry is very precise and coats of arms were usually given to individuals, who might or might not have had the right to pass them along to descendants. There may well be a given family with your surname who's entitled to a coat of arms, but simply having the same name doesn't mean it applies to you. In fact, the odds are that it doesn't. And I hope I'm not disappointing anyone, but those "family histories" they offer? Not yours. Just a generic collection of random tidbits that they'll sell to anyone who happens to sport your surname.

Again, I'm not suggesting that you ignore all those stories Grandpa told you. Even with the ones that have grown grander over the generations, there was likely a very real person or event that sparked the tale, so they're definitely worth checking out. Consider this a chance to sharpen your detective skills. Think of family lore or any suspicious or unsupported information as a hypothesis and then try to prove or disprove it through your research.

THE NAME GAME

I used to work a lot in developing countries where all sorts of unexpected things can happen. For instance, it was a routine occurrence for the power to go out in the middle of a presentation. A friend of mine referred to these little episodes as "another opportunity to exercise flexibility." Genealogy also offers plenty of opportunities to exercise flexibility—especially about your surname.

Many people are convinced that they have the only true version of their name, one that has existed just as it is forever. As the online rep for an ethnic society, I was often called upon to help folks who were hoping to find their old world cousins so they could meet them during the trip they had coming up in three or four weeks. Not the best of circumstances, but I did my best to assist. Time and time again, I would pick up the family's trail in records—let's say a census record showing the immigrant couple and their twelve kids (usually spaced with impressive regularity every two years). The family would be in the correct location and everyone would have the right first names and ages, but the person requesting the help would respond that this wasn't their family because the last name was spelled differently.

If you limit yourself to searching only records that match your exact and current spelling, you will undoubtedly miss some of your family. This might seem fairly obvious for surnames like my own that invite misspelling, but this can happen even with the most simple of names. When Bob Hope, born Leslie Townes Hope, was to be honored by Ellis Island some years ago, they ran into a little snag. He couldn't be found in the passenger arrival records even though it was well known he had come here in 1908. A quick look revealed that he was there, transcribed in the searchable database as Leslie Hape. If you look at the original record, the transcriber did an accurate job. It could easily be read as

Hape. But that was all it took to keep this future national treasure hidden from view.

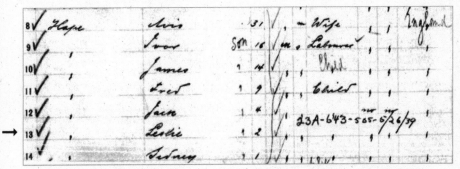

Future comedian Bob Hope arrives at Ellis Island as Leslie "Hape" in 1908 with his mother and siblings. *(courtesy of Ancestry.com)*

Now imagine that your name is Motyczka or Menecola. Can you see where others could get creative with it? Or even family members could opt for different spellings? My husband has uncles who spell our name Smolenak and Smolenyak, and they're American-born brothers raised in the same household. If you'd like to amuse yourself, you might even want to start a collection of all the variations of your name you find over time. My collection is quite extensive, so I've included just a sampling on page 18.

Incidentally, this flexibility should also be employed when dealing with first names and old country towns of origin. John in America might have been Johann, Janos, Jean, or countless other variations originally, and if your family hails from Abbeyfeale, Ireland, you'll do yourself a favor to be open to Abbeyfeall, Abbeyfeele, Abbyfeale, Abbeyfiale, Abbyfoale—you get the idea.

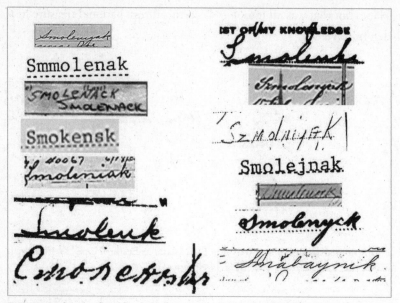

Be prepared to be flexible about how your name is spelled. Here's a selection of the collection of Smolenyak spellings I've found in assorted documents. *(courtesy of the author)*

SURROUND AND CONQUER

It's one aspect of Murphy's Law that the ancestor you're seeking will be the one whose life was completely undocumented or whose records were destroyed in natural disasters and fires. For this reason, it's good practice to research not only your direct line forebears, but also collateral lines. In other words, if you can't find Great-Grandpa, maybe you can find his brothers and sisters and use their records to backdoor into the information you're looking for. I find this to be especially true when it comes to efforts to identify the birthplace of an ancestor.

Maybe your great-great-grandfather, Olaf Andersson, came to America before the place of birth was routinely provided in passenger arrival records, but his brother Nils made the journey a decade later, and his record happily does include that information. If you can't find out where Josephina Miller came from in Germany, maybe an affidavit in her brother's Civil War pension file will furnish the missing detail. Almost all our ancestors' paper trails are spotty, but paying attention to siblings and cousins can often fill your gaps.

Relatives of your ancestors are the most obvious people to research, but if you find yourself truly stuck, it can help to think of other associates. Maybe his neighbors, fellow parishioners, or classmates can help you get closer. It's not at all unusual, for instance, to discover that neighbors came from the same place in the old country or are relatives of some sort. Our ancestors often traveled in packs of people they were comfortable with.

When it comes to finding the living—say, you want to find out who in your extended family wound up with the family Bible—you might want to get even more creative. I've located people by contacting the Model A club they belonged to, or in one case, deliberately calling someone of the same name in the same town. I couldn't reach the one I wanted, so I purposely called the wrong one. She knew who I was talking about because they went to the same vet. As it happened, they both had Chihuahuas, so their records were always getting mixed up. Because of this coincidence of names and dogs, they had come to know each other. Deliberately calling the wrong one put me in touch with the correct one.

LEAVE A TRAIL OF BREAD CRUMBS

One of the admittedly less thrilling but important aspects of genealogy is citing your sources. A source is any document, database, interview, or other resource that provides a nugget of information in your quest. Yes, I know, the very thought might make you flash back to school days spent painstakingly creating footnotes and endnotes for your papers. And the elements are more or less the same—author, title, publication details, location, and specifics (see the appendix for more). But getting into this habit early will make you a better researcher and save you and others unnecessary effort.

There are definite parallels between genealogy and detective work, and one of them is the central role of evidence. Think of *CSI* and *Law & Order*. A major portion of every show is devoted to the gathering of evidence, and what's the first thing detectives do when they find something? They protect, label, and log it. They must do this whether the particular piece of evidence they've just found supports or contradicts their working theory, and ultimately, to build a compelling case that will convince others and stand up in a court of law. Unless you become an heir searcher, your research isn't apt to take you into a courtroom, but shouldn't you care enough about your sleuthing to be sure you're right and be able to prove to your kinfolk that your latest discovery is accurate?

You might think early on that you can remember it all—where you got this or that bit of information—but as you add more newly found relatives to your database, you'll quickly realize that it's simply not possible. One day, you'll find yourself staring at a great-grandfather's date of death with no clue how you came across this information or how reliable it might be. Did you get his death certificate, interview his last surviving child, find it on a random Web site, snag his obituary, or see his tombstone? Where did you find it and can you trust it? His son, your great-uncle, might have seemed certain when he gave you the date off the top of his head, but is it possible his memory could be a little off? Might it be worth verifying with some other sources, just to be sure it's correct?

Failing to cite your sources also causes you to reinvent the wheel. You could easily find yourself ordering the same marriage record two or three times because you didn't record it the first time. And you'll inevitably encounter some situations that send you mixed signals. Three documents indicate that your immigrant ancestor was born around 1873, but his baptism from the old country has him born in 1869. Which is right? If you cited all your sources, you'll be able to weigh the reliability of each one against the others and reach a reasoned conclusion—and so will your cousins and descendants. Think how frustrating it would be for your great-great-grandkids to come across your database a hundred years from now but not be able to follow your trail. Make it easy on yourself and them. Get into the sprinkling-bread-crumbs habit from the very start.

TELL, DON'T DWELL

At some point in your family history, you will probably encounter a hint of scandal. Or maybe a boatload of it. We seem to pride ourselves on having invented vice, but the truth is that our ancestors were just like us. Some were noble, hardworking, accomplished, and worthy of emulation. Many were decidedly average. And some were total schmucks. I count my great-grandfather who abandoned his wife and kids in Eastern Europe, only to marry my great-grandmother seven weeks after landing in America, in this last category.

What do you do with these black sheep? My personal policy is tell, don't dwell. I don't believe in whitewashing history, but I also don't feel the need to make a movie of the week out of these ancestors or events. What happened happened, and it's interesting to see how often something considered shocking a century ago becomes ho-hum or even admirable over time.

Richard Murphy, the eldest son of a pair of my Irish immigrant ancestors, married an African American woman in the 1880s. As a result, he was so thoroughly scrubbed from the family tree that I didn't discover him until every-name census records (more on these later) became available for all states and census years. All of a sudden, the great-granduncle I assumed had died young seemingly materialized in another state. Additional records proved that he was indeed the fellow

I thought he was, and there he was with his "mulatto" wife. As I shared news of this recovered branch of our family tree with relatives, the typical reaction was along the lines of, "Huh, that's interesting!"—probably a little different from the reaction Richard got from the family at the time.

Most families either hide or celebrate their black sheep. The problem with wiping them out of existence is that they can become an obstacle in your research. If you don't know that Great-Granddad went off to prison and disappeared after he was released, you may never find out about his second family and all the half-cousins you have out there. So my bias is to bring them out of hiding without making a major issue of them, but you'll have to decide what you're comfortable with. Should you need more help wrestling with this issue, I suggest you check out the International Black Sheep Society of Genealogists (www.ibssg.org/blacksheep) run by flockmaster Jeff Scism. Be sure to take a look at the rather entertaining list of qualifications, and if the scandal in your family is fairly recent, consider joining the Tender Lambs Corner.

GENEALOGY

As your tour guide into the world of genealogy, I feel somewhat protective of you, so I want to impart one last piece of advice: Genies—me included—can occasionally be just the tiniest bit snarky. If you'd like to test this out, find any sort of family history forum and post a message that includes "geneOlogy." Then run for cover!

The word is pronounced as if it had an "o" in it and this classic misspelling is so widespread that some have made money off of Web sites that deliberately used this incorrect version. But that doesn't stop it from irritating folks. In general, genealogists are among the kindest, most generous people out there, but there's something about changing that "a" to an "o" that brings out the Hulk in us. So save yourself some avoidable needling by mastering the spelling of your new pursuit.

GET YOUR SHERLOCK ON

While I've highlighted a handful of potential pitfalls here, please don't let them overly concern you. I'm just trying to shorten your learning curve so you're able to fill out the branches of your family tree as quickly as possible. As you get into your family history, you'll quickly come to regard these hiccups as just another opportunity to get your Sherlock on. There's something oddly satisfying about outwitting a distorted spelling or poor transcription, and don't be surprised to find yourself saying "Gotcha!" out loud as you corner an elusive ancestor in the census. Before you know it, you'll delight in swapping tall tales about how you cleverly stitched together the clues that solved your family history mystery. So now that you're equipped, let's move on to the amazing, online world of family history.

2

WEBBING IT: WHAT'S ONLINE?

I t's truly astonishing how much of our collective past has been uploaded over the last few years, even if it represents only a tiny fraction of what might eventually be in store for us. Chances are that you'll be stunned as you start wading through the billions of records that may hold pieces of your puzzle.

Still, it's wishful thinking to suppose that everything you might want to find about your family is online. In fact, a March 2009 *New York Times* article calculated that at the current pace, it would take the National Archives 1,800 years to digitize its text collection, much less any of its other holdings—and that's just one of countless repositories that might contain snippets of your ancestors' lives. Having said that, there's more than enough already available to make the Internet the next logical stop once you've scoured your home and pestered your older relatives for clues.

In the chapters that follow, we'll explore different types of records that family detectives turn to time and time again, but first, we'll take a tour of some of the Web sites that should be high on the list for your online adventures. There are so many—believe it or not, genealogy is often cited as ranking up there with porn and finances in terms of online popularity (it seems that "sex and drugs and rock and roll" have been supplanted by sex, money, and roots)—that it would be impossible to cover even a fraction of them.

It was very difficult to decide which to include in this chapter, and inevitably, I will receive rebukes about those not included here. Those you-forgot-this-one challenges will be well founded as there are many I've reluctantly excluded. For that reason, it might be useful to briefly explain the logic behind my choices. Because this book is mainly about American genealogy, I gave preference to Web sites that also have that focus. Several wonderful U.K.-centered resources, for instance, aren't here for that reason—though we'll definitely be exploring immigration-related sites since America is a land of immigrants. I also aimed for diversity of content and purpose so new genealogists could sample a number of options on the family history menu. Knowing how much we all value convenience, I've limited myself to resources that can be accessed at home, which means that a few excellent ones that are available only on-site at libraries are absent from this group. To give myself a touch of wiggle room, I "cheated" a few times and created a category into which I could toss more than one Web site. And finally, in the case of tough calls, I simply asked myself which I turn to over and over. Since I practically live online and get to flex my research muscles on a daily basis, that seemed as good a tiebreaker as any.

The ones we'll cover here range from massive sites that house millions of family trees and billions of records to one-man shows that help you zero in on what you're looking for faster. Some are free, while others are fee-based (hint: some of the fee-based ones can be accessed free at your library or even remotely at your home through your library membership). Many are overflowing with records containing your ancestors, while others are designed to educate, connect, entertain, or direct you to the countless other Web sites that can't be squeezed into the pages of a single book. And for good measure, I'll include the fellow who gets my vote for funniest genealogist on the planet.

ANCESTRY.COM

If, for some reason, I were forced to choose only one Web site to use for American genealogy, Ancestry.com would be it. Experienced genies appreciate Ancestry for its *billions* of searchable, digitized records including the ones we turn to most often—census, military, immigration, etc. Once you get into ancestor-hunting, you develop an insatiable appetite for records, and no site feeds that hunger better than this one.

But it's also the best starting place for "newbies," the term generally used for those taking their first steps in genealogy. That's because it's been designed with them in mind. Ancestry.com doesn't assume that users arrive knowing exactly what they're looking for. If you're new to family history research, you may never have heard of a census record, so how would you know to look for one? Ancestry makes the process as intuitive as possible.

When you first visit the site, you're invited to start a family tree, beginning with your own name. You'll need to register, but there's no fee. To give you an idea how popular these online trees are, over 10 million pedigrees with more than a billion individual profiles have been added to Ancestry in just two years.

You'll be guided step-by-step to enter what you know about yourself, your parents, your grandparents, and so forth. If you don't know certain details, you can guess. For instance, if you think your grandfather was born around 1900, enter that year to get started. The system is smart enough to know that you might be estimating.

Look at part of my personal tree on Ancestry.com and you'll notice a couple of things. First, you're seeing faces. That's because I've uploaded images and attached them to people in my tree, and while you're seeing photos here, anything that can be scanned can be added. Tens of millions of images have been uploaded by Ancestry users—partly because these trees are a great place to collaborate with your far-flung cousins.

A portion of my Ancestry.com member tree with photos and Ancestry hints. *(courtesy of Ancestry.com and the author)*

Inviting them to your tree and encouraging them to go through their albums and shoeboxes is an easy way to ferret out and reassemble those treasured photos and documents that were dispersed around different branches of your family.

The other thing you might have noticed are little leaves to the right of some of the names. These are Ancestry hints, although many call them "shaky leaves" because they pulsate slightly when they first appear. These indicate that possible records have been discovered for your ancestors. Based on the information you enter—any combination of names, dates, and places—the billions of records on Ancestry are searched for matches. When you click on the leaves, you can view the records and accept or reject each clue presented. It's like having a personal research assistant who digs through all the databases and other members' family trees for you.

Incidentally, this is where a subscription fee kicks in. Anyone can host a family tree, invite their relatives, and upload images and audio (accomplished by entering your phone number, speaking into your phone when it calls, and hanging up) for free, but accessing and attaching records from Ancestry.com requires a subscription. The site offers both domestic and international options. If you'd like to take it for a test drive, visit your local library as most provide free access to the majority of Ancestry.com's databases.

Speaking of databases, there are presently about 28,000, although that figure is constantly climbing. Vital records, newspapers, yearbooks, draft registrations, federal and state census records, maps, county histories—whatever you can think of, you're apt to find. Many genealogists use Ancestry purely for this incredible record set that can be searched in a variety of ways.

Ancestry.com also offers a learning center with videos and webinars, multiple ways to collaborate with others, MyCanvas so you can publish books and charts of your discoveries (a great gift, by the way), and DNA testing. To cover it all would require its own book, which is why you might want to consider snagging a copy of *The Official Guide to Ancestry.com* by renowned genealogist George G. Morgan.

FAMILYSEARCH.ORG

At the moment, this is a trio of Web sites—FamilySearch.org, pilot .FamilySearch.org, and beta.FamilySearch.org—that are in the process of morphing and will eventually merge back under the FamilySearch .org umbrella, quite possibly by the time you're reading these words (as of the writing of this book, digitized records are presently found on the pilot and beta versions and will be cited here with pilot.FamilySearch .org addresses, but please be aware that you will find everything at FamilySearch.org at some point). These Web sites are a service provided by the Church of Jesus Christ of Latter-day Saints, known by many as Mormons. It's part of the Mormon faith to "redeem the dead," meaning to bring them into the Church through a sort of vicarious baptism. In order to do this, it's necessary to research one's ancestors, and for that reason, the Church has become the largest repository of genealogical records in the world. Fortunately, these records are available to all. So extensive is this granite mountain–protected collection that it's not unusual for foreigners to travel to the Family History Library (FHL) in Salt Lake City because records for their home country are easier to search there.

FamilySearch.org and its pilot companion are the online doors to this cornucopia of family history records. The FHL has only recently begun placing digitized records online, and though that process is going at a breakneck pace, what's found on the Internet will remain the proverbial tip of the iceberg for some time to come because of the sheer volume of the collection. For that reason, it's important to familiarize yourself with the Family History Library Catalog. At the moment, this catalog is reachable on FamilySearch.org by selecting the Library tab and then Library Catalog from the drop-down menu, but a Web 2.0 version is expected to be launched shortly. This is where you can search—by place, surname, keyword, title, and other options—more than 2.4 millions of rolls of microfilmed records. Once you find what you're looking for, you can have it delivered to your closest Family History Center (there are over 4,500 around the globe), hire someone in Salt Lake City to get the record for you, or travel there yourself (genies love dreaming up excuses for trips to Utah).

The pilot.FamilySearch.org site (also reachable through the "search records" menu on FamilySearch.org), which already sports millions of records and indexes, is random, but impressive and growing fast. Some are browsable (meaning you can click through and look around page by page), while others are completely searchable (meaning you can go directly to the entry for a person of interest). A massive volunteer transcription effort is gradually converting browsable records into searchable ones, and a large portion of the collection is digitized. For genies, this is a candy store.

A sampling of what's available includes Ohio death certificates (1908–1953), Ellis Island Arrival Lists (1892–1924), Vermont Probate Files (1791–1919), Massachusetts State Census (1855 and 1865), and San Francisco, California, Funeral Home Records (1835–1931). Emphasis at present is on census and vital records, but as you can see from the preceding, there are plenty of other documents. Depending on your heritage, you might also benefit from the international nature of the site. Looking for marriages from the Philippines, burials in Norway, the 1895 Argentina census, or Civil Registration indexes for Ireland? You're in luck. New content is added so frequently that it's worth checking on a weekly basis.

These Web sites are completely free, and in many cases, you'll be able to print out, save, or download the record you seek on the spot. And thanks to a friendly user interface, you'll find it easy to do so.

CYNDISLIST.COM

Cyndi Howells is a rock star in the genealogical world. Just as many would be challenged to tell you Cher's or Madonna's surname, the same is true of Cyndi because she's attained that one-name stature. Mention Cyndi to any genealogist in the world and they'll instantly know who you mean.

The reason for this is www.cyndislist.com, a collection of well over a quarter of a million links to online genealogical resources organized into more than 180 categories. What started as a personal set of bookmarks went live in March 1996 and has evolved into a remarkable card catalog of everything genealogical you could possibly think of. Whether your ancestors were Loyalists, Lutherans, or from Luxembourg, Cyndi has a category of links that will steer you exactly where you need to go to learn more.

People have a hard time believing this, but Cyndi's List is homegrown and maintained. She updates it on a daily basis and personally inspects every Web site before assigning it to the appropriate category. Those that have not yet been vetted can be found under "New and Uncategorized."

It's fun to browse the topics from "Clothing and Costumes" to "Serendipity," but the true strength of Cyndi's List is revealed when you find yourself asking, "Now where would I find out about . . . ?" Discovering an ancestor who came from Barbados, for instance, you'll be delighted to find her Caribbean/West Indies section.

This is a site you'll never outgrow, so you'll want to bookmark it. Even the most seasoned professionals find themselves consulting it on a frequent basis. And in case you're curious: no, Cyndi hasn't had much time to research her own roots since 1996. She's too busy helping all of us with ours.

USGENWEB AND ROOTSWEB

One of the best ways to tackle your research is geographically. Many of us have ancestors who roosted in this or that state or county for several generations. Under ideal circumstances, you can travel there and visit local libraries, cemeteries, courthouses, and so forth. But that's not always possible. Fortunately, there are kind-hearted volunteers across the country who have shared bits and pieces of just about every locality's past online, and there's a decent chance that a few of your forebears are mentioned.

Both USGenWeb (www.usgenweb.org) and RootsWeb (www.rootsweb .ancestry.com) are volunteer-based initiatives that provide free resources for the genealogical community. Though they offer other content, I turn to them primarily to home in on what's available at the local level. USGenWeb is organized mainly at the state level, while RootsWeb is more county-focused. Because the home page for RootsWeb has a long menu of links, I find it easiest to get to the relevant county by Googling "rootsweb" and the name of the county and state (some county names are found in multiple states).

What you'll find is random, but frequently worthwhile. Many localities are extremely well maintained and contain bounties of family history information. You might find databases of vital records, cemetery transcriptions, military indexes of local men who served, county histories, maps, and more. For this reason, it's good practice to check for your states and counties of interest and search for your family's surnames (and once your research takes you beyond the United States, you might also want to visit WorldGenWeb.org). But because USGenWeb and RootsWeb are both volunteer-driven, there are naturally some gaps, so you should expect to occasionally come across a location that's been more or less abandoned with no fresh content added for years. If that happens, maybe down the road you could consider being the kind soul who adopts and revitalizes the orphaned locale.

FOOTNOTE.COM

Footnote is a relative newcomer, but already a big hit with genies. It's content-rich, loaded with millions of documents—what every family historian craves. This subscription-based site has a user-friendly interface that's both intuitive and fun, allowing you to mouse over portions of a page to learn more or to interact with historical documents by adding your own annotations. You might add a short note to offer an alternative spelling, but some users create whole pages, appending letters an uncle wrote while serving in World War II, photos, or other gems. This participatory aspect is so popular that it's easy to get distracted and lose a few hours wandering through others' discoveries and contributions.

The content is a mix of historical documents and newspapers including everything from Revolutionary War service records to FBI case files. History buffs will enjoy meandering, browsing correspondence from George Washington, Custer's court-martial, and even UFO investigations. And those with ancestors who served at any time in America's history are apt to find plenty to like since it's heavy on military papers.

Footnote can be searched by name, keywords, state, and titles (record sets), but also invites users to explore by historical eras, ranging from Revolution (1700s–1815) to PostWar (1950–2000s). Because of all this, I find it hard to discipline myself and retrieve a particular record as I almost always stumble across something else that I can't help but investigate. To avoid this peril, you might want to set a time limit when you sign in.

GENEALOGYBANK.COM

Newspapers are a treasure trove and GenealogyBank is all about newspapers. I suppose I should qualify that by acknowledging that it also serves up a generous helping of historical documents and the Social Security Death Index (more on this in chapter 4), but it's the impressive newspaper collection that draws most researchers to this fee-based site.

Genies love newspapers because they help us get past the basic birth-marriage-death information and bring our ancestors to life—and journalists from days gone by could be quite free with their opinions about your forebears. As to more recent newspapers, genealogists have an ongoing love affair with obituaries. That might sound a tad twisted, but once you have your first experience with an obit that's ripe with family details, you'll understand.

Largely overseen by genealogy guru Tom Kemp, this master collection is notable in terms of both its time and geographic coverage. The digitized Historical Newspaper collection extends all the way back to 1690, so is a tremendous resource for those with colonial roots. America's Obituaries, by contrast, is far more contemporary, starting in 1977 and having its greatest concentration over the last decade or so. And while the number of newspapers varies, all states are represented, so you've got a chance of spotting a few ancestors regardless of where your family once lived.

> Died in Jamaica, Mrs. *Mills*, aged 118; she was followed to the grave by 205 of her children, great-grand-children, and great-great-grand children, sixty of whom, named *Ebanks*, belong to the regiment of militia for St. Elizabeth's parish. For 97 years she practised midwifery, during which period it is stated that she ushered 143,000 persons into the world! She retained her senses to the last, and followed her business until within two days of her death.

An article found in several July 1805 newspapers in Genealogy-Bank's Historical Newspapers collection. If this was all true, Mrs. Mills would have an impressive number of descendants, and Jamaica would be really crowded! *(courtesy of GenealogyBank.com)*

The Historical Documents portion of the Web site is also worth a look. I recently turned up a list of people making claims for luggage lost when Ellis Island burned in 1897. If your grandparents happened to be among them, that would certainly add a dash of spice to their arrival-in-America story.

ELLISISLAND.ORG AND CASTLEGARDEN.ORG

Approximately 40 percent of Americans have at least one ancestor who took their first steps in the United States at Ellis Island, and many of us have several, so the fact that a large portion of the records for this port are digitized and available online free is good news (you'll need to register, but there's no cost). This database has more than 20 million arrivals for the period from 1892 (when Ellis Island opened) through 1924 (when immigration was on the wane, partly as a result of legislation that tightened restrictions), so there's a good chance you'll be able to spot a relative or two.

The Mormon Church (mentioned earlier in the FamilySearch section) orchestrated the efforts of twelve thousand volunteers who donated over 5.6 million hours to create this database offered online by the Statue of Liberty–Ellis Island Foundation. Launched in 2001 when such collections were something of a novelty, it promptly crashed because of unanticipated demand, but was quickly reinforced.

Ellis Island records, especially those after 1906, can be very helpful in identifying a place of origin in the old country. In addition, these manifests usually provide details such as age, occupation, birthplace, last residence overseas, the name and address of a relative in the old country, the name and address of another relative (or sometimes friend) in the United States, and the final destination of the traveler. It can also be an eye-opener to learn how little money your ancestor arrived with.

A similar and slightly overlapping site called Castle Garden (www.castlegarden.org) is also worthy of exploration. It includes indexes from 1820 to 1913, but the bulk of its content predates 1892. This collection has few digitized images, but the information furnished can be used to obtain a copy of the record from other sources.

Both the Ellis Island and Castle Garden Web sites can be challenging

to search because of creative spelling and other factors, but www
.SteveMorse.org (more on this site shortly) is a useful finding tool that
will help you unearth those stubborn ancestors-in-hiding. Ellis Island
records are also searchable at Ancestry.com and pilot.FamilySearch.org,
described earlier.

GOVERNMENT

Most of what the federal government provides online for genealogists
comes in the form of finding tools and research assistance rather than
databases. That may well change in the future (some agencies are part-
nering with private companies to make their records available on the
Internet because of the significant investment required), but for the
moment, government Web sites serve more as stepping-stones than final
destinations. Still, you're shortchanging yourself if you don't check out
what they have to offer.

The two most deserving of your attention are the National Archives
and Records Administration (NARA) and the Library of Congress.
The National Archives just celebrated its seventy-fifth anniversary,
and its largest constituency is genealogists. I frequently consult www
.archives.gov/genealogy to learn more about assorted record sets, where
they're located and how to access them. NARA's Web site is a great
place to soak up much of what you might want to know about census, military, immigration, naturalization, land, passport, and other
records. You'll also find insightful articles and tutorials, instructions
for ordering records, and yes, even several dozen electronic (mostly
military-oriented) databases, some of which contain millions of entries
(although few scanned images).

You could easily lose track of time clicking around the Library of
Congress Web site, but I'd suggest you start with American Memory
(http://memory.loc.gov/ammem/index.html). American Memory looks
deceptively simple, but houses an astonishing array of manuscripts,

photos, maps, videos, and other treasures that can be searched by topic, time period, or location. While it may be difficult to find specific mentions of your ancestors (but you never know—it's worth a try), this collection is compelling because of the context it can supply. Check out the Dust Bowl, Slave Narratives, Chinese in California, or Civil War Photographs topics, just to name a few. With more than a million images, American Memory is an excellent starting point for those wishing to walk in an ancestor's shoes.

Chronicling America (http://chroniclingamerica.loc.gov/), an initiative centered on historic American newspapers, is also worth a browse. Currently, it contains free, digitized images for a selection of newspapers from a dozen states for 1880 to 1922. But beyond that, it also helps you track down just about every newspaper in America dating back to 1690. Looking for nineteenth-century newspapers from Jersey City, New Jersey? This site can tell you exactly which seven repositories contain part or all of the *Jersey City Daily Times* from 1864 to 1868.

GOOGLE

In recent years, Google has truly become a genealogist's friend. Sure, you can search for an ancestor's name and hometown, and possibly trip across a fun find. Most of us would know to give that a try. But click on the More option at the top, select Google Books, and do a little searching there. You might be rewarded with books or articles authored by your ancestors or mentions of them in others' works.

During a recent can't-sleep-so-I-might-as-well-surf session, I was startled to stumble across the answer to a decade-old question.

> April 8th.—David Nelligan, aged 8, went under the gate at Grove street crossing, Jersey City, at 8:55 A.M., and attempted to run across the tracks in front of N. Y. and G. L. train 18 (J. M. Hoffman, conductor; engine 5, Wm. Howard, engineer); he was struck by the engine and received injuries from which he died shortly after being brought to St. Francis Hospital.

Google Books accidentally solved a family mystery for me.

A youngster had disappeared from my family back in the 1800s, but while I assumed he had probably died young, I had never been able to find out what happened. Randomly entering some surnames and locales from my family tree, I came across a description of his accidental death in 1889 in the *Annual Statements of the Railroad and Canal Companies of the State of New Jersey*—a resource I was entirely clueless about and never would have thought to consult even if I had heard of it.

Google's News Archives (news.google.com/archivesearch) is also very useful for genealogists. Though called "News Archives," it searches not just newspapers, but other resources (such as some of Ancestry.com's databases), and will indicate whether any given result is free or involves a fee. Genies particularly like the Timeline feature, which can help you zero in on articles from or pertaining to a specific period. You'll find a mixture of contemporary and historical coverage, so you might find your ancestors, but don't be surprised to spot yourself as well.

This is admittedly the briefest of introductions, so determined researchers wishing to extract every last clue that Google might hold to their family's past would be well advised to get a copy of *Google Your Family Tree* by Dan Lynch.

LIBRARIES, ARCHIVES, AND SOCIETIES

I've made references to the Family History Library in Salt Lake City and the Library of Congress, but there are many other libraries, archives, and societies (genealogical, historical, lineage, and others) that deserve your attention. Which ones will be most valuable for you will depend largely on the specifics of your heritage (though it's almost always worth joining a local society—even if your ancestors are from elsewhere—just to find like-minded souls). The quantity and quality of what they offer online varies widely, but here's a sampling of some of the better-known ones you may wish to acquaint yourself with:

- New England Historic Genealogical Society (NEHGS) (www.newenglandancestors.com)

- Allen County Public Library (www.acpl.lib.in.us/genealogy and www.genealogycenter.info)
- National Genealogical Society (NGS) (www.ngsgenealogy .org)
- Southern California Genealogical Society (SCGS) (www .scgsgenealogy.com)
- Ohio Genealogical Society (OGS) (www.ogs.org)
- The New York Genealogical & Biographical Society (NYGBS) (www.newyorkfamilyhistory.org)
- Daughters of the American Revolution (DAR) (www .dar.org)

For those with New England ancestry—especially the many Americans with colonial roots—NEHGS, founded in 1845, hosts a number of databases that can expedite your research. Its library in Boston and the Allen County Public Library in Fort Wayne, Indiana, are among the top genealogical destinations in the United States. In fact, I'd say that most serious American genealogists would list Salt Lake City, Washington, D.C. (because of the National Archives, Library of Congress, DAR, and other repositories), and Fort Wayne as their top three choices for family history field trips, with Boston not far behind. In addition to all the other resources and services they provide, NGS, SCGS, and OGS all host some of the largest annual genealogy conferences in the country. Established in 1869 and 1890, respectively, NYGBS and the DAR are among the oldest and most respected societies.

To find other societies that may be especially relevant for you, go to the Federation of Genealogical Societies (www.fgs.org) and click on the "great organizations" link. Because they're mostly state-specific, I didn't include any archives above (note: some states combine their libraries and archives, while others keep them separate), but quite a few furnish online databases and other resources. They're not the tidiest of Web addresses, but both of the following will take you to links you can scan and investigate for whichever states your ancestors may have

settled in: www.dpi.wi.gov/pld/statelib.html and www.cyndislist.com/
lib-state.htm#States.

ETHNIC

Regardless of your heritage, there's a Web site for you. In fact, there are
probably several or even dozens. I happen to be half Carpatho-Rusyn,
and I'm willing to bet that most reading this have never heard of
this ethnicity (hint: we're from the Carpathian Mountains in Eastern Europe and our big claim to fame is that Andy Warhol was one
of us). And yet, there are Web sites for us. I can join the Carpatho-
Rusyn Society or check out the Carpatho-Rusyn Knowledge Base,
Carpatho-Rusyn Genealogy Web site, or Slovak and Carpatho-Rusyn
Genealogy Research Pages.

So imagine if you're, say, African American, Irish, Jewish, or German.
If you're of African heritage, you may well know of AfriGeneas.com
(derived from *Afri*can American *Genea*logy Buddie*s* and pronounced
A-fri-GEE-nee-as). This decade-old Web site has an amazing array of
records, forums, articles, chats, and links and consistently appears among
the "best of the Web" lists. Similarly, if you have any Jewish ancestry,
you'll want to spend hours exploring all the corners of JewishGen.org,
which hosts a mind-blowing selection of databases (many of them the
result of heroic effort by dedicated volunteers) and a variety of discussion
and special interest groups, projects, and other resources.

But how do you find the ones most relevant to your roots? You can
Google, of course—entering your ethnicity and "genealogy"—but you'll
probably find what you're looking for faster if you start at Cyndislist
.com, mentioned earlier. Either use the search field in the upper right
or browse the indexes on the left. Alternatively, you can go directly to
www.cyndislist.com/searchit.htm. Be sure to set aside time for some
serious surfing, though, as it's easy to lose track of time clicking around
all the possibilities.

MAGAZINES

One of the best ways to shorten your learning curve is to subscribe to one or more hard-copy family history magazines. While there are many publications to choose from, those just getting their feet wet will probably be most interested in the ones geared toward hobbyists, rather than professionals. Fortunately, there are several that are simultaneously entertaining and educational, and also have an online presence.

You won't go wrong with *Ancestry Magazine* (www.ancestrymagazine .com), *Family Tree Magazine* (www.familytreemagazine.com), and *Family Chronicle* (www.familychronicle.com). All three are lifestyle magazines and include a lively mix of how-to articles, case studies that read more like mystery stories, related topics such as roots travel and scrapbooking, and updates on the latest resources at our disposal. Web sites for all of the magazines provide free access to a variety of archived articles, so you can sample them before subscribing (or grab a copy during your next jaunt to your local bookstore). *Ancestry* and *Family Tree Magazine*'s sites toss in other extras, such as blogs, downloadable forms, and community forums.

If you subscribe to any, don't be surprised to find yourself monitoring the mail, taking the newly arrived issue, and slipping off for a little me-time to swallow it down. It may soon become one of your not-so-guilty pleasures.

ROOTSTELEVISION.COM

RootsTelevision.com is an online channel with hundreds of free videos "by and for avid genealogists and family history lovers of all stripes." Searchable and available 24/7, the site features over twenty categories of shows. As cofounders Megan Smolenyak[2] (guilty) and Marcy Brown explain, "These days, there's a horse channel, a wine channel, a sailing channel, a poker channel, a guitar channel, and even a shipwreck channel. So why, we wondered, isn't there a channel servicing the millions of people interested in genealogy and family history? . . . Whether you're an archives hound, a scrapbooker, a cousin collector, a roots-travel enthusiast, a Civil War re-enactor, a DNA fan, a reunion instigator, a sepia-toned photos zealot, an Internet-junkie, a history buff, an old country traditions follower, a cemetery devotee, a storyteller, a multicultural food aficionado, a flea market and antiques fanatic, a family documentarian, a nostalgia nut, or a mystery-solver, RootsTelevision .com has something for you."

New videos—ranging from interviews conducted at genealogical conferences to original programming—are added weekly on New Roots Tuesdays (to keep up on the latest, subscribe to the blog or newsletter). Popular shows include *DNA Stories*, *Down Under* (about "stories beneath the stones" in cemeteries), and *Unclaimed Persons* (genealogists helping coroners). RootsTelevision.com also allows viewers to upload videos they'd like to share with fellow roots enthusiasts through RootsTube, a family history version of YouTube.

Incidentally, videos can be watched full-screen, and if you're the kind who prefers to watch shows on conventional television sets, a simple cable hookup between your laptop and TV will allow you to do so. Check the Help page to learn how.

ISOGG.ORG

One of the most exciting developments in family history over the last decade has been the addition of DNA to our research toolbox. We'll explore this in a later chapter, but in the interim, you might want to consider joining the International Society of Genetic Genealogy (ISOGG—pronounced eye-sog). Founded in 2005, it already has over six thousand members from roughly sixty countries—and it's free. Rather refreshingly, the Web site informs visitors, "There are no membership dues. There are no donations accepted. Your money is not wanted by us, so go spend it on a DNA test."

ISOGG is a terrific resource for those getting their feet wet in the world of genetic genealogy (check out the site's "Newbies" section), as well as a playground for those who find themselves addicted. So well respected is the young organization that DNA testing companies are adopting their recommended standards, an impressive show of respect by scientists for "amateur" genealogists.

The group is spearheaded by the tireless Katherine Hope Borges, and offers mailing lists (including one for newbies), speakers, success stories, videos, and even a page dedicated to famous DNA (in case you're curious whether you might be related to Jesse James or the Romanovs). Want to learn more about specific testing companies such as DNA .Ancestry.com, FamilyTreeDNA.com, and 23andMe.com? Post a query and you'll get an earful. A smart way to familiarize yourself with genetic genealogy is to subscribe to ISOGG's newsletter and browse past issues. You'll find that they're written in plain English and make for enjoyable reading.

STEVEMORSE.ORG

Steve Morse was the architect behind the development of the 8086 chip for Intel. Put another way, he's one of the reasons we have PCs today. Luckily for the genealogical world, this brilliant gentleman decided to lend his talents to the realm of family history.

Back in 2001 when the Ellis Island site first came online and crashed under the weight of the demand for its records, Steve was one of those who set his alarm for three a.m. to get in when traffic was lighter. But even so, he was frustrated by his inability to find the arrivals of his wife's grandparents. He decided to create a search form to facilitate his Ellis Island queries, and quickly found his prey—though he couldn't understand why his wife wasn't as excited as he was when he woke her up one morning at four o'clock to share the good news!

Steve thought others might benefit from the form, so he popped it online, and it wasn't long before genealogists struggling to find their ancestors latched on to it. What he had done was make it possible to search using different spins on names (e.g., starts with, sounds like, etc.), a tremendously helpful feature since so many are hidden under unexpected spellings and transcriptions. He also added a number of criteria (such as year of birth, year of arrival, and name of ship) so you could narrow your search if you were coping with a common name or lucky enough to have a few details of Granddad's arrival. Try out his Ellis Island Gold Form to get a feel.

Though he's still much revered for his Ellis Island contribution, it turned out that this was just Steve's debut. He now travels the gene-alogy circuit speaking on a variety of topics, but what he remains best known for is his ability to make Web sites more searchable than they were originally designed to be.

SteveMorse.org (emphasis on *.org*, as .com will take you to a rock-er's site and likely leave you perplexed) has evolved into a remarkably diverse set of search forms for a cross-section of Web sites pertaining to immigration, census, naturalization, and vital records (those who share Steve's New York City roots will find even more to like), as well as an eclectic mix of calendar, translation, and other tools. While you're there, why not check for any relatives lurking in New York Incarcera-tion Records?

FINDAGRAVE.COM

My husband is what's referred to as an NGS—nongenealogical spouse. He has an impressively high tolerance for living with a wife who's long overdue for genie rehab, but he's not a genealogist himself. So I think it says something about this Web site that it's one of his favorites, though he enjoys tormenting me by insisting on calling it "PickA-Grave." I think there's a good chance it will become one of your favorites as well.

As the name suggests, it's a massive database of graves—mostly transcriptions, but many with photos of actual tombstones—intended to help you find the graves of your ancestors. I would give you the count, but the figure changes so rapidly that whatever I write would be out of date by next week, so suffice it to say that FindAGrave contains tens of millions of names. You'll find plenty of famous people, but many more ordinary folks, and occasionally, this is the only resource that had just the clue I needed.

The content comes entirely from volunteers. They may add their own family members, those buried in the cemetery near their home, military vets from across the country, or only the notable and notorious. Everyone has their own preference, but collectively, it adds up to one very useful site. I find it intriguing to peruse the profiles of the top fifty contributors to see what motivates them. As of this moment, it takes more than 58,000 entries to get you into this elite club, so these folks are serious.

Most search the site by name and state, but you'll find entries for Canada, England, Ireland, and some other countries mixed in. You can also zero in on a particular cemetery, which can be very handy as our ancestors were much more likely to have shared a plot than we are today. At major metropolitan cemeteries, a single plot can easily include ten or so family members, and may be your best means of discovering children who sadly died young. Even co-located ancestors from different branches often wound up in the same graveyards, particularly if they attended the same church or shared a common ethnicity. For this reason, finding one great-great-grandfather and browsing the other entries for that cemetery will often lead to additional relatives.

To get a sense of FindAGrave, you might want to try searching for

Lucille Désirée Ball of *I Love Lucy* fame. If you do, you'll find two listings because her family had her disinterred from California and reburied in New York where she was originally from. Between them, you'll see more than five thousand remembrances left by fans. Most graves have only a few such notes, but they're often from relatives of some sort, so they're worth browsing if you find listings for your own ancestors. For that matter, you might want to leave remembrances (being sure to include your relationship and e-mail address) to help unknown cousins find you in the future. I suspect there have been quite a few virtual reunions among living descendants of people now "residing" at FindA-Grave, and there's no reason you shouldn't be next.

DEATHINDEXES.COM

Genealogists are often accused of being more interested in the dearly departed than in the living, and I have to admit that there's an element of truth to this assertion. But the reality is not as morbid as it—or this Web site—might sound. It just happens that those who came before us can be fascinating, and uncovering their death dates can often be the key to opening up the rest of their lives. The death date and location might lead you to a tombstone that gives your third great-grandmother's maiden name or an obituary that reveals that the fellow you were named after served in the War of 1812. Now you can pick up her trail as a child and his in military records.

I suppose that's why Joe Beine created DeathIndexes. Joe's territory extends to a handful of topics (see www.deathindexes.com/sites.html for links to census, military, immigration, and other online resources), so be sure to explore, but somewhat ironically, it's DeathIndexes genealogists can't live without.

When you visit, you'll see that it's a clean, no-nonsense site. As Joe explains, it's "a directory of links to websites with online death indexes, listed by state and county. Included are death records, death certificate indexes, death notices & registers, obituaries, probate indexes, and cemetery & burial records." It's so simple that you may be deceived, but start clicking around and you'll soon begin to understand the Web site's popularity.

Select a state of interest and scroll down the page. His tidy lists each start with statewide resources, then regional ones (say, if several county library systems join together to create a shared obituary index), then county-specific links, and, when appropriate, city-level ones. The user is often bounced to a dedicated page for major metropolitan areas.

The vast majority of Joe's links steer you to online resources, though he takes the time (usually toward the end of a list) to mention some that are found offline. He also lets you know when links require payment. It impresses me that one person can find all these links and manage to keep them current, and I'm grateful that Joe does. By the way, in case you're curious (I was), his last name is pronounced By-nee.

Online Illinois Death Records & Indexes

A Genealogy Records Guide

Online Illinois Death Indexes

- Illinois Death Index 1916-1950
- Illinois Death Index pre-1916 for only a few counties - more will be added
  - List of Counties Presently in the pre-1916 Index includes Cook County death index 1871-1915
- 1929 Illinois Roll of Honor Database contains the burial locations of 72,000 Illinois veterans

- Illinois Newspaper Obituaries Archive includes recent obituaries for 100 IL newspapers, mostly from the 2000s, but some date back to the 1980s & 1990s (requires payment for full results - you can obtain online copies of individual obituaries for a fee)

- Adams County: Quincy Public Library Historical Newspaper Archive 1835-1919
- Adams County: Greenmount Cemetery Burials in Quincy, IL (not complete)
- Boone County Cemeteries
- Boone County Historical Society Museum Obituary Search
- Brown County: Index to Cemetery Burials 1825-1921
- Cass County Deaths 1878-1915
- Clinton County GenWeb Site includes Deaths December 1877-1950, St. Dominic's Catholic Church Death Records 1858-1927 (in Breese, Illinois), cemetery listings, and other indexes
- Coles County: City of Mattoon Death Certificate registers Index 1899-1918
- Coles County: Dodge Grove Cemetery Records (Mattoon, Illinois)
- **Cook County & Chicago...**
  - The Cook County section has moved to its own webpage...
    - Chicago & Cook County Death Indexes, Records & Obituaries
- DeWitt County GenWeb Site - includes a Death Index 1878-1917 and other indexes
- DeWitt County Coroner's Inquest Files Index 1924-1977
- Du Page County: Wheaton Vital Records Database January 1885-July 1887 from the Wheaton Public Library (includes births, marriages & deaths)
- DuPage County Cemetery Records

DeathIndexes.com is organized by state, region, and county and is loaded with useful links. *(courtesy of Joe Beine)*

DEADFRED.COM

First FindAGrave, then DeathIndexes, and now DeadFred. Right about now, you might think that I have a peculiar obsession, but this site—in spite of its name—has nothing to do with mortality. Click on "Meet Fred" if you're curious about Fred, but this is a "genealogy photo archive" run by Joe Bott. I think of it as a photobase—a database of photos.

Photographs are a valued component of genealogy. Though most living today have probably been photographed more times than they can remember (think of our poor descendants having to plow through our digital libraries in the future), we're only a few generations removed from those who were lucky to leave any such traces. For that reason, genealogists love photos. It thrills us beyond belief to finally see what Great-Grandpa looked like (I know I felt that way when it happened to me).

But photos can also be frustrating. Even if you have them, many of our short-sighted ancestors neglected to label them, leaving you to guess who the handsome fellow in the bowler hat was. And they tend to stray. An elderly relative passes away and the estate management company sells all the family memorabilia. By the time you hear, it's too late (am I the only one who finds herself wondering whose relatives those sepia-toned faces on restaurant walls are?).

DeadFred allows us to indulge our love of photos and rescue them as well. The Web site serves as a sort of middleman, helping pictures get to those who will appreciate them most or in front of those who might be able to identify the mystery people staring out from them. You can upload your own or search others' (by name, location, etc.) to see if perhaps a distant cousin posted one of a shared ancestor. And if you're one of the fortunate ones, you might trip across one of your own ancestors. To date, there have been about 1,500 reunions. In fact, I was one of them.

Back when the site first launched, I was asked to write a review, so I tested it by posting a mystery image from my own collection. It shows half a dozen children in costumes (apparently a class play) and was taken around the 1910s. I knew that someone in my family was in it, but that's all I knew, so I put it on DeadFred, noting that it was from Jersey City and had been owned by my grandmother, Beatrice Agnes (Reynolds) Shields.

I wrote the article and forgot about it until I received an e-mail about six months later from someone saying she also had Reynolds ancestors from Jersey City. I didn't get terribly excited until I read the rest of the message, and it became clear that the writer was descended from the first family of an immigrant ancestor of mine, James Reynolds. I had only recently discovered that he had this other family (I was descended from his youngest, Charles, affectionately known in the family as "last chance Charlie" because he was born when James was seventy), and they found me because of my little experiment. The photo remains a mystery, but I reclaimed a lost branch of my family, so I count myself among DeadFred's success stories.

RANDOM ACTS OF GENEALOGICAL KINDNESS (RAOGK.ORG)

Wouldn't it be terrific to have a network of thousands of volunteers scattered across the country (and maybe a few other countries) to help whenever what you're looking for—say, a picture of the tombstone of that third great-grandfather you just discovered who died in Massachusetts in 1833—is out of reach? You already have it. Just surf your way to www.raogk.org, read the guidelines, go to the page for the relevant state, and scroll to find a volunteer in the county where your ancestor lived.

You're asked to keep your request reasonable (no "Can you research my Smith family?" inquiries) and reimburse for expenses incurred (such as copying). Since the volunteer is working for free and may have a backlog of requests, you might have to exercise a little patience. And every once in a while, you might not get a response. Perhaps the volunteer you contacted is on vacation or otherwise indisposed.

All these caveats are necessary when dealing with any kind of volunteer organization, but my personal experience has been extremely positive. For example, I've twice made requests for obituaries from Hawaii—at different times from different researchers—and both copied the obit and scanned and e-mailed it to me within twenty-four hours. By RAOGK guidelines, they're required to reply within forty-eight hours to two weeks, but being avid genealogists themselves, sometimes the volunteers can't resist the urge to go digging immediately.

BLOGGERS

It started around 2004. With the exception of a few pioneers like Leland Meitzler (www.genealogyblog.com), there were hardly any genealogists blogging before that time. Now it's become a bit of an epidemic with well over 1,300 genies blogging their hearts out. To search for ones that might trip your trigger (perhaps you're keen on cemeteries, Polish roots, or humor-oriented blogs), check out the Genealogy Blog Finder from Chris Dunham (aka The Genealogue): www.blogfinder.genealogue.com.

In case you don't feel like swimming through hundreds of blogs, here are a few of the best and most popular to get you started:

- Eastman's Online Genealogy Newsletter (www.eogn.com): Dick Eastman's blog, which he describes as "The DAILY newsletter for genealogy consumers, packed with straight talk—hold the sugar coating—whether the vendors like it or not!"
- About.com Genealogy (www.genealogy.about.com): Kimberly Powell's insightful and educational writings on just about everything genealogical ever.

- Dear MYRTLE (www.blog.dearmyrtle.com): The alter ego of Pat Richley, one of genealogy's best-informed and most-beloved professionals.
- The Genealogy Guys Podcast (www.genealogyguys.com): A frequent and newsy podcast by George G. Morgan and Drew Smith to help keep you up on the latest happenings in the genealogical world.
- The Ancestry Insider (www.ancestryinsider.blogspot .com): Thoughtful and thorough analysis of many genealogical topics provided by a gentleman who prefers to remain anonymous.
- The Genetic Genealogist (www.thegeneticgenealogist .com): Written by Blaine Bettinger, this is the go-to

Top Ten lists like this are just one of the ways The Genealogue makes genealogists laugh at themselves. *(courtesy of Chris Dunham)*

resource for those wishing to stay current on the field of genetic genealogy.

- Genea-Musings (www.geneamusings.com): Randy Seaver's blog that explores and comments on just about every aspect of genealogy, frequently provoking a "me, too" or "I was wondering that" response from its countless readers.
- The Genealogue (www.genealogue.com): If you subscribe to no other blog, subscribe to this one. Chris Dunham is hands-down the most hilarious genealogist alive (and no, "hilarious" and "genealogist" are not mutually exclusive). The more you get into researching the roots, the more you'll come to see yourself in his laugh-out-loud postings. But watch out for his "exclusives," which are written in such a convincing faux-journalistic style that many fall for whatever he says no matter how outrageous it is. He once had folks thrilled about a supposedly 129-year-old woman!

SOCIAL NETWORKING

If 2004 was the year the blogging trend began in genealogy, 2008 was the year genies went mad about Facebook, and 2009 ushered in Twitter-mania. For whatever reason, MySpace hasn't caught on in the genealogical world, but if you're looking for family history playmates, you can find plenty of them on Facebook and Twitter. To join us, simply go to Facebook.com or Twitter.com, sign up if you haven't already (it's free), and search on genealogy, family history, and similar terms (while you're there, go ahead and "friend" or "follow" me).

This is a great way to network with fellow enthusiasts and keep up on what's happening in genie-land. Those who attend conferences, for instance, will tweet often so those who can't be there can follow along and get a sense of the event. At some gatherings, you can even spot the occasional iPhone battle where genealogists are racing to be the first to post photos. But if you're a tad wary of these sites and prefer to learn more before diving in, you'll find Drew Smith's *Social Networking for Genealogists* a helpful primer.

There's also another form of social networking for genealogists that's more directly family-focused. If you want to play the six-degrees-of-separation game and try to round up as many distant cousins as possible, you might want to give one of the following a spin:

- WeRelate.org
- Geni.com
- MyHeritage.com
- OneGreatFamily.com

These are all useful for playing global games of tag and can be a handy way to keep in touch with your extended family. Some, like WeRelate, are sophisticated and designed with serious genealogists in mind, while others, such as MyHeritage, offer fun toys like the ability to upload your photo and see which celebrities you most closely resemble. Or perhaps you'd prefer to upload your child's photo along with yours and your spouse's to see which of you your son or daughter favors more. In terms of expanding your family tree, though, it's good to exercise a touch of caution when these services seek to link or merge yours with others', as it's easy to take a misstep by, say, confusing two individuals who happened to have the same name. It's great to add a bunch more names to your family tree, but not if they're not really your family.

HAPPY SURFING!

As I said at the outset of this chapter, it's not all online yet. And that's good news because there's something pretty magical about skulking

about musty archives and discovering a document that was once actually held by your ancestor. But somewhat paradoxically, although only
a minuscule fraction of what's of value to genealogists resides on the
Internet, that fraction is already a mother lode for us. I hope that some
of the Web sites profiled here will initiate you into the battalions of
early-morning pajama surfers.

3

LEARNING TO LOVE THE CENSUS

Are you one of those who tosses your census forms in the trash or turns out the lights and pretends not to be at home when the census taker rings your bell? If so, your descendants will curse you. They would "curse your name," as the expression usually goes, but if you successfully eluded the census, they might not be able to find out what it was.

Census records are a genealogical gold mine bursting with clues. Conducted every ten years (going back to 1790) in the United States, they provide snapshots of family units in time. There's your grandfather as a toddler in the 1930 census with his parents, siblings, and—bonus—his grandmother! Now you've learned his parents' names and even a little about the generation before them. Go back another ten years, and there's your *great*-grandfather with *his* parents and siblings.

If your family's been here that long, you stand a good chance of being able to steadily march your way back as far as the 1850 census. Before that, it gets more challenging, since only the heads of household are listed, but still, census records are a great way to dash back a century or more.

Because they're so comprehensive (the 1930 census alone has roughly

123 million people in it), furnish so many details about our ancestors, help link generations, and are widely available, census records are work-horse documents that many take their first steps with and return to frequently. So let's get started.

TALKING CENSUS

Many think of the census in political terms because of their use in defining congressional districts. The Census Act of 1790—signed by none other than George Washington—established a constitutional requirement for the federal government to take a count of the population every ten years. In the early years, they were essentially glorified head counts, but starting in 1850, the government began gathering additional information to gain insight into employment, education, housing, health, and other issues.

Genealogists are the accidental beneficiaries of all this counting. There was never any intention to record our forebears for posterity, but that's exactly what happened. Fortunately, most of the records have survived, so now we get to virtually peek into the windows of our ancestors' lives and even households. Due to privacy restrictions, records are made public after seventy-two years. Family historians rejoiced when the 1930 census was released on April 1, 2002 (I was one of many at the National Archives in Washington, D.C., that day itching to get my hands on those records), and are counting down the days until the 1940 set is made public.

As just mentioned, census records are available at the National Archives—both in the nation's capital and at regional branches around the country—and can also be found in other repositories such as the Family History Library in Salt Lake City, Utah, and the Allen County Public Library in Fort Wayne, Indiana. But in recent years, they've also become available online, and though there are occasions for in-person research using microfilm, surfing the Web is easier and more convenient. At this moment, you can find some or all of the federal census on:

- Ancestry.com (all of it; fee-based except at libraries)
- Pilot.FamilySearch.org (free; 1880 and growing portions of other years)
- Footnote.com (1930; fee-based)
- HeritageQuest (accessible through libraries only)

For a long list of links to other census bits and pieces scattered around the Internet, visit www.cyndislist.com/census.htm.

The only Web site that has a complete set of digitized images for the entire census, as well as every-name indexes for every year, Ancestry.com's coverage is the most comprehensive, so many avid researchers subscribe to it directly. Both Ancestry.com and HeritageQuest can be researched free at most libraries, and you might be able to gain remote access at your home to HeritageQuest through your library membership.

DECADE BY DECADE

What exactly can you learn from census records? The answer depends on the year. In a nutshell, the farther back in time you go, the less information you can expect to glean. The 1790–1850 censuses are light on details and only include the name of the head of household; 1850 is a banner year because it's the first to record the names of all the residents in a household; 1860 and 1870 offer up a couple of extra tidbits, but 1880 is another leap forward with lots of helpful family details; 1890 is a genealogical heartbreaker because most of it was destroyed in a fire, but the situation got brighter in 1900 and continued to do so up through 1930. We'll look at each period in more detail starting with the earliest days of our country.

1790–1830

These early census records include only the names of the heads of house-holds. Everyone else is recorded more as a statistic, lumped into categories by gender and age groups. And of course, the census was only conducted in the states that existed at the time (so no 1790 records for Hawaii), and some of them are missing. For instance, in 1790, you'll find records for Connecticut, Maine, Maryland, Massachusetts, New Hampshire, New York, North Carolina, parts of Pennsylvania, Rhode Island, South Caro-lina, and Vermont, but not for Delaware, Georgia, Kentucky, New Jersey, Tennessee, and Virginia. The reason? The latter were destroyed during the British attack on Washington, D.C., during the War of 1812.

Luckily, most census records survived over the years, and you can consult a publication called *1790–1890 Federal Population Censuses* on www.archives.gov for a state-by-state account of what's available.

Even with seemingly skimpy information such as that provided in these early censuses, it can be fairly easy to trace your family back through the decades, especially if your ancestors had names that were slightly unusual. Heads of households of "free colored persons" were also included, which is helpful for those descended from the approxi-mately 10 percent of African Americans who were free before Emanci-pation. With a little methodical comparison of household profiles (that is, paying close attention to age and gender groups over time), it's often possible to pluck your family out decade after decade, even for those with more common names.

With a little practice, there are other ways you can "work" these early census records to unearth more clues. Census takers weren't required to work in any particular order, but it made life easier for them to record people living near one another all at once. Because of this, examin-ing those listed within a few pages of your family might help you spot possible relatives, since our ancestors had a tendency to cluster near kin. Obvious candidates are those with the same surname and in likely age ranges to be siblings or parents. If your ancestor Thomas Farley is recorded next to another Thomas Farley with older family members indicated in the age categories, you've found a possible father-son or perhaps uncle-nephew relationship to investigate.

Incidentally, the 1830 census was the first to provide standard printed forms to the census takers, introducing a degree of uniformity that makes searching them a tad easier than the earlier ones. Prior to that, those involved used whatever paper they had.

1840

The 1840 census still only included heads of households, but tossed a few new questions into the mix. Now census takers—sometimes referred to as enumerators—notched the number of individuals in school, over age twenty-one who could not read and write, those who were deaf, dumb, blind, and "insane" (according to the understanding of that time), and in certain industries (agriculture, manufacturing and trade, navigation of the ocean, etc.). But the bonus that's most appreciated is the names and ages of Revolutionary War pensioners (veterans or their widows), useful information for those hoping to link their family to this landmark chapter in our nation's founding.

A cluster of Revolutionary War pensioners recorded in Pittsford, Vermont, in 1840. *(courtesy of Ancestry.com)*

1850

As the first to list all individuals by name, the 1850 census is a significant milestone for family historians. Age, gender, and birthplace were also recorded, as well as other details such as occupation and whether an

Chang & Bunker	38	m	Farmer	4,000	Siam
Eng Bunker	39	m	"	"	Siam } Twins
Sarah A. "	27	f			North Carolina
Adalade "	20	f		"	
Catherine "	6	f			"
Josephine "	6	f			"
Julia A. "	5	f			"
Christopher "	5	m			"
Decator "	4	m			"
Nancy "	3	f			"
James "	2	m			"
Mary A. "	7/12	f			"
Patrick H. "	7/12	m			"

Chang and Eng, the original Siamese twins, were farmers in Mount Airy, North Carolina, in 1850. Note that the column on the right correctly records their birthplace as Siam. *(courtesy of Ancestry.com)*

individual married or attended school within the year. Although relationships are not stated, it's usually possible to make educated guesses based on the information furnished. An older woman in a household, for example, was likely the mother of one of the parents. Using simple logic, if she had the same last name as the husband, she was probably his mother, but if she had a different surname, she was likely the mother of the wife. It's important not to overassume—an elderly woman with a different last name could also be the husband's mother who remarried after being widowed—but most of your theories of family relationships formed on these records are apt to be correct.

The 1850 census is also notable for the introduction of separate slave schedules. The number of slaves owned (and freed) is given for each slave owner. While slaves are unfortunately not listed by name, the records indicate age, gender, and color of all slaves. This information can be invaluable when trying to piece together pre-Emancipation generations of families that were enslaved.

This particular census is often referred to as the first modern one, not only because of the additional data gathered, but because of how it was done. This was the first time that printed instructions were given to the enumerators, not surprisingly resulting in greater consistency and accuracy than in previous years. It spelled out, for instance, that census takers had to personally make contact with every family and dwelling, thereby minimizing shortcuts, such as asking neighbors or even making details up. This doesn't mean that such problems evaporated entirely, but the quality of the 1850 and more recent censuses undoubtedly improved because of these standards.

It's also worthy of note that 1850 reflected America's expanding geography with the inclusion of nine new states and territories: California, Florida, Iowa, Texas, Wisconsin, Minnesota, New Mexico, Oregon, and Utah.

1860

The 1860 census is quite similar to its immediate predecessor, but was the first to include estimates of personal estates, which can give you a glimpse into your ancestors' financial standing. Census takers were also instructed to be more specific about birthplaces, so those of German heritage, for instance, might learn which state (Prussia, Baden, Bavaria, etc.) immigrant forebears originally came from.

Slave schedules show that Chang and Eng owned eighteen slaves in 1850. *(courtesy of Ancestry.com)*

1870

The 1870 census ushered in several improvements. Columns were added to indicate whether parents were of foreign birth, a handy detail for identifying immigrants. For those born or married within the previous year, the month is given, which can be helpful for tracking down associated records, such as a child's baptism or birth registration. And new race categories—Indian and Chinese—were incorporated.

As the first post-Emancipation census, 1870 is also the first to list former slaves by name. The "wall of 1870" is a frequently heard expression in African American genealogy and refers to the ability to research African American roots back to this census before hitting what genies call a "brick wall." It can also be useful for scouting out possible former slave owners, since many stayed nearby, at least initially. This is important because identifying owners is often a critical first step in knocking down the wall of 1870.

This census is also used by many (usually in conjunction with the 1860) to get a first take on ancestors who might have fought in the Civil War. If an ancestor of an appropriate age to have been a soldier appears in both the 1860 and 1870 censuses, he may have participated and survived. If he's in the 1860, but absent from 1870, he may well have lost his life in the conflict. Either situation could have generated a paper trail, such as military service and pension files, that will reveal much more about your family.

1880

Looking at your ancestors' record in the 1880 census almost feels like peering into the window of their house. That's because this is the first in which street and house numbers were noted, not to mention relationships and marital status. Starting in 1880, the census gives you a clear picture of all the residents in a dwelling and how they're connected to one another. No more guessing about whether that mysterious older gentleman in the house might be a father-in-law, uncle, boarder, or servant. The record will spell it out for you.

If your great-great-grandmother is the head of the household, you'll be able to tell whether that's because she was widowed or divorced, and that's an important clue in terms of determining what happened to your great-great-grandfather. If his spouse was widowed, you'll know to research his death sometime in the 1870–1880 time period, but if she's listed as divorced, you'll know to keep looking for him elsewhere in the 1880 census.

Another welcome addition in 1880 is the birthplaces of everyone's parents. This information can give you a sense of your family's migration. If you find them in Ohio in 1880, the parents' birthplaces might point you to Virginia, Pennsylvania, or New York to pick up the trail in earlier years. Or they might reveal that you've hit the immigrant generation as your ancestor's parents were listed as being born in England. Parents' birthplaces—especially when an unexpected combination, such as China and England or Vermont and New Mexico—can make it easier to find your family in census records for other years since online databases sometimes include fields to search on spouse's and parents' birthplaces. Particularly when you're dealing with a common name like Smith, Williams, or Jones, entering such tidbits of information can be just what you need to narrow the field and make your family stand out.

Yet another modification is the recording of the number of months unemployed within the last census year, and whether sick or temporarily disabled (as well as the reason). While this won't help with tracing your

The 1880 census shows author Samuel L. Clemens, better known as Mark Twain, with his family and German, Irish, and African American servants in Hartford, Connecticut. (courtesy of Ancestry.com)

family over time, snippets of information like these help bring your ancestors to life by revealing challenges they encountered and coped with.

1890

This is the census genealogists mourn the loss of. Fire and water damage
caused by a fire in the Commerce Department in 1921 resulted in the
destruction of more than 99 percent of this census (a little more than six
thousand names survived), but there are some work-arounds. Ancestry.
com, the National Archives, and the Allen County Public Library have
developed (and continue to add to) a census substitute. On Ancestry.com,
you'll find the remaining portion of the actual 1890 census, special 1890
veterans schedules (including Union vets and widows for the District of
Columbia, half of Kentucky, and all states in the alphabetical range from
Louisiana to Wyoming), Native American tribe censuses conducted close
to 1890, state censuses recorded in 1885 and 1895, city directories for
the late 1880s and early 1890s, voter registration documents around this
time, and other records. All told, more than 20 million names have been
cobbled together. It's not as satisfying as seeing your whole family enumerated in a single dwelling, but it's a huge step forward to filling what
would otherwise be a significant gap from 1880 to 1900.

1900

One of the reasons genies love the 1900 census is that it's the only one
to report both the month and year of birth of our ancestors. Even the
ones that came later didn't include this information. Granted, it isn't
always correct, but it seems that being forced to specify a month caused
at least some of our ancestors to reflect and give a more accurate answer
than they might have otherwise.

It's also handy to have for comparison purposes when trying to find
relatives in the World Wars I and II draft registrations (covered in chapter 5). If you find, say, five candidates of the same name in the expected
location in the World War I draft records, you can compare birth dates

given in the 1900 census and the draft registration. If your grandfather is listed as having been born in May 1895 in the 1900 census, then you know to look for a fellow with a corresponding birth date in the World War I records.

The 1900 census is also the one in which important information about immigrants was first collected. Year of arrival and years in the country are recorded, as well as whether an individual had been naturalized. These are critical clues for finding your ancestors in immigration records, especially since so many arrived during what's thought of as the Ellis Island

Name	Relation			Birth					Birthplace
Keller Kate	Head	W	F	Oct	1840	59	Wd	3 3	Arkansas
— Helen A	Daughter	W	F	June	1880	19	S		Alabama
— Mildred C	Daughter	W	F	Oct	1886	13	S		Alabama
— Phillips B	Son	W	M	July	1891	8	S		Alabama
King Robt	Servant	W	M			45	S		Scotland
Keller Simpson	Step Son	W	M	Feb	1874	26	S		Alabama

			Occupation				
Massachusetts	Vermont		Landlady		yes	yes	yes
Alabama	Virginia		At School	9	yes	yes	yes
Alabama	Arkansas		At School	9	yes	yes	yes
Alabama	Arkansas		At School	9	yes	yes	yes
Scotland	Scotland	Un	Garden labour	0	yes	yes	yes
Alabama	Alabama		Civil Engineer	6	yes	yes	yes

As occasionally happens, Helen Keller appears in the 1900 census twice. The record above shows her on June 25 with her family in Tuscumbia, Alabama, while the following one shows her on June 1 with her teacher, Annie Sullivan, in Cambridge, Massachusetts. Note that the enumerator for the second one made the remark "B.D." on the right—most likely indicating "blind, deaf." *(courtesy of Ancestry.com)*

Name	Relation			Birth			
Fosdick Sarah W.	Head	W	F	Nov	1860	39	S
Sullivan Annie M.	Lodger	W	F	July	1868	32	S
Keller, Helen A.	Lodger	W	F	June	1880	19	S
Bacon Mary	Lodger	W	F	Sept	1877	22	S
Moore Charlotte L.	Lodger	W	F	Mar	1874	26	S
Lloyd Margaret M.	Servant	W	F	Jan	1851	49	S
Cronin Bridget W.	Servant	W	F	Jan	1856	44	S

			Occupation								
Massachusetts	Massachusetts		Lodging House Keeper	0	Yes	Yes	Yes	R	14		8
Ireland	Massachusetts		Teacher (deaf)		Yes	Yes	Yes				9
Alabama	Arkansas		Student		Yes	Yes	Yes				10 B.D.
New York	Missouri		Student		Yes	Yes	Yes				11
Massachusetts	Massachusetts		Student		Yes	Yes	Yes				12
Ireland	Ireland	1864 39	Cook		Yes	Yes	Yes				13
Ireland	Ireland	1870 30	House maid	0	Yes	Yes	Yes				14

era starting in the early 1890s. Don't be too literal about the years provided, though, as your ancestor's memory may have faded. If the census indicates that he arrived in 1899, it's a good bet that it's accurate since that was the previous year, but if it says 1850, he may be guesstimating.

Starting with the 1900 census, you can learn whether your family owned or rented their home, if it was mortgaged, and whether it was a house or a farm. All of this fleshes out their lives a bit. Still more valuable insight into the lives of your great-greats may be found in the addition of questions about the number of years married, children born to the mother, and children still alive. The first can help you narrow the time frame when looking for a marriage record, while statistics about children can often be startling as they tend to bring home the harsh reality of how many of our ancestors' offspring died young. Don't be surprised, for instance, to discover that your great-grandmother had nine children, but only two were still alive at the time of the 1900 census. On the other hand, if the census indicates that she had five children still alive, but only three were listed with her, that's a signal to look for other children—perhaps older ones who had already married and moved out. Because the 1900 census ends the twenty-year gap since the 1880 census, it's quite common for children to have been born, married, and disappeared in this window of time (especially since they married younger then), so the discrepancy between the number of children alive and those in the household is often your only hint that you're dealing with missing siblings. For all these reasons, the 1900 census is regarded much like the 1850 and 1880 in that they all introduced new elements that family historians appreciate.

1910

This census is very similar to the previous one, but offers more information about immigrant ancestors, specifically whether they were naturalized (na), alien (al), or had applied for papers (pa). It's also handy for those with Civil War ancestors as there's a column that indicates

The 1920 census (split above; left half on top, right half on bottom) showing eighteen-year-old Walt Disney living with his brother's family and already working as an artist/cartoonist. The "OA" on the far right means he worked on his "own account." In other words, he was self-employed. (courtesy of Ancestry.com)

whether an individual was a survivor of the Union or Confederate army or navy.

1920

The 1920 census was both a step forward and a step backward. On the one hand, it's the only census to include a question asking an immigrant's exact year of naturalization, which can be extremely helpful in locating that person's naturalization records. It also asked the mother tongue of each individual and his or her parents. But unlike 1910, the 1920 census no longer included questions about Civil War military service, the number of children, or the duration of marriage.

1930

The 1930 census is the one most genealogists will first use, perhaps looking up some combination of themselves and their parents, grandparents, and great-grandparents. So it's fortunate that it's one of the more interesting. Veteran status returned to the census, including an indication of which war(s) a man served in. Also added was the value of your ancestor's home or the monthly mortgage or rent. The age of first marriage is another welcome detail that can make it easier to find marriage records or a hint of a previous marriage. But the detail that seems to captivate most is whether their ancestors owned a radio. In 1930, radio ownership suggested you were reasonably well off and the kind who kept up with newfangled technology.

FOR CENSUS JUNKIES

If you're the kind who always wants to know more and is hungry for every detail possible, here's an admittedly clunky Web address where you can look up precisely which questions were asked for each census from 1850 (the first year written instructions were provided to the census takers): http://usa.ipums.org/usa/voliii/tQuestions.shtml. Perhaps the best synopsis ever done of census information over the years can be found on page 170 of *The Source: A Guidebook to American Genealogy*, edited by Loretto Dennis Szucs and Sandra Hargreaves Luebking. Those wishing to learn how to research census records on microfilm at the National Archives, Family History Library, Allen County Public Library, and other repositories will also find ample guidance. For serious genealogists, this is one of the classics and easily one of the most-consulted resources in the field. Take a peek the next time you're at the library, treat yourself to a copy, or explore the version that's recently been placed online at www.ancestry.com/wiki.

And finally, if you simply must have a more recent census record (the 1940 will be released to the public on April 1, 2012), you may be able to order an official transcript in the interim. See www.census.gov/genealogy/www/bc-600.pdf for more details and an application form.

SPECIAL AND STATE CENSUSES

But wait! There's more! While most of your census research will be focused on federal population schedules, there are some other schedules and censuses you might want to explore once you've covered the basics. These include:

- 1885 Federal Census—Colorado, Florida, Nebraska, and the territories of Dakota and New Mexico took advantage of an opportunity to conduct an interim census partly funded by the federal government.

- Mortality schedules (1850–1885)—Censuses for these years listed the names of most of those who died during the previous year, valuable information at a time when few states were recording deaths. Other details usually provided are sex, age, color, whether widowed, place of birth, occupation, month of death, and cause of death.

- Agricultural schedules (1850–1880)—If any of your ancestors were farmers, these schedules can tell you about their land, livestock, and crops. Although they were kept up to 1910, the more recent ones were destroyed by fire or an act of Congress.

- Manufacturing schedules (1820, 1850–1880)—As with agricultural schedules, these won't tell you the specifics of your ancestors' lives, but can give you a sense of the businesses they might have run with details such as the type of product and number and wages of employees. For both agriculture and manufacturing schedules, only farms and businesses above a certain threshold are included.

- Veterans schedules (1840 and 1890)—As mentioned earlier, the 1840 federal census can point you to ancestors who served in the Revolutionary War, while the surviving portion of the 1890 census of veterans of the Union Army can do the same for Civil War survivors (or their widows).

- Slave schedules (1850–1860)—Briefly addressed previously, these special schedules in the two censuses leading up to the Civil War can be key for those seeking to identify onetime owners of enslaved ancestors in order to research pre-Emancipation generations.

- Native American Censuses (1885–1940)—Though not comprehensive, many with Native American ancestors living on reservations during this period will find multiple mentions of them in this record set.

Many states also conducted their own censuses that were prior or complementary to the federal ones (often in the years ending with 5, though there are plenty of exceptions). Such records are less accessible than the federal ones because they are scattered in assorted repositories, random in their coverage, and mostly lacking an index. Having said that, a growing number can be found (indexed) on Ancestry.com and pilot .FamilySearch.org, as well as at state archives and libraries and the Family History Library and its many centers. Pages 205–206 of *The Source* (as well as the online version available at www.ancestry.com/wiki), cited earlier, include a list of state census schedules from 1623 to 1950.

SEARCHING THE CENSUS

We've considered the various census records available in advancing chronological order, but since you start with yourself and work backward in genealogy, most of your sleuthing is apt to be in reverse. To get a feel for this, we'll walk through a typical search.

Since we just took a peek at Walt Disney's 1920 census, let's stick with a Disney theme and say that you're researching a relative who happened to share the name of one of his most famous characters, Snow White. And though you're not sure of her birth and death dates, you know that "your" Snow White lived during the past century. Since Ancestry.com has the most comprehensive census collection, we'll try a search there.

Based on the results, it turns out that Snow White wasn't the most

Search Census & Voter Lists Records

☑ Exact matches only   Search tips

First & Middle Name(s)   Last Name   Spelling
snow   white   Exact ▾

Lived in   State
USA ▾   All States ▾

Year range
[   ] to [   ]
e.g. 1827 to 1903

Search

Searching census records for Snow White in the United States. *(courtesy of Ancestry.com)*

unusual of names. I could have restricted the search more by entering time period or location details, but less is often more when dealing with databases. Each detail you enter is searched, so if, say, a sloppy census taker incorrectly noted the birth state of your ancestor, you could end up with "no results found" if you include that state as one of your cri-

🗋	11	1930 United States Federal Census
🗋	10	U.S. IRS Tax Assessment Lists, 1862-1918
🗋	8	1910 United States Federal Census
🗋	7	1900 United States Federal Census
🗋	7	1920 United States Federal Census
🗋	3	1880 United States Federal Census
🗋	2	1850 United States Federal Census
🗋	2	1891 England Census
🗋	2	Florida State Census, 1867-1945
🗋	2	Kansas State Census Collection, 1855-1925
🗋	1	1860 United States Federal Census
🗋	1	1870 United States Federal Census
🗋	1	U.S. Indian Census Schedules, 1885-1940

Search Results
Census & Voter Lists

Preliminary search results for Snow White in U.S. census records. *(courtesy of Ancestry.com)*

teria. This happens often enough that I tend to start with broad searches and narrow them as necessary if I get too many hits.

In this case, the results are manageable—one to eleven hits in perhaps a dozen databases. Eyeballing them, I can rule out quite a few. The years 1850–1870 are too early, I don't need the 1891 in England, and perhaps I know she wasn't Native American, so can eliminate the Indian Census. Since we start with the most recent and work backward,

View Record	Name	Parent or Spouse Names	Home in 1930 (City,County,State)	Estimated Birth Year	Birthplace	Relation	View Image
View Record	Snow White	James	School District 45, Roosevelt, MT	abt 1886	Montana	Son	
View Record	Snow White	Leata	Oklahoma City, Oklahoma, OK	abt 1886	Oklahoma	Head	
View Record	Snow White	Simeon R, Ella David	Selma, Fresno, CA	abt 1899		Daughter	
View Record	Snow N White		Watertown, Jefferson, WI	abt 1901	Missouri		
View Record	Snow L White		Claremont, Dodge, MN	abt 1904	Minnesota	Cousin	
View Record	Snow White	Clarence, Pearl	Nashville, Howard, AR	abt 1913		Daughter	
View Record	Snow White		Watters, Floyd, GA	abt 1915	Georgia	Boarder	
View Record	Snow White	James A, Esther	Lafayette, Crawford, AR	abt 1921		Daughter	
View Record	Snow Lee White	Crawford	Louisville, Jefferson, KY	abt 1923		Daughter	
View Record	Snow White	Oscar	Brewer, Howard, AR	abt 1926		Daughter	
View Record	Snow White	Wesley, Gladys	Bristow, Randolph, AR	abt 1926		Granddaughter	

Snow Whites in the 1930 U.S. census. *(courtesy of Ancestry.com)*

I would likely decide to dive in with the 1930 census, which apparently includes eleven Snow Whites.

Scanning the basic information in the results presented, I can see that I'm dealing with Snow Whites born between 1886 and 1926, born everywhere from Montana to Georgia, and now living in eight different states. I might also register the random fact that Snow White was apparently a more popular name in Arkansas than in other states, but let's say that I know that the Snow White I'm looking for lived in California. I'm in luck! There's just one. With a couple of clicks, I can view a digitized image of her 1930 census record.

Thanks to this single record, I can see that Snow was born to Simeon and Ella in Kansas. It could be that I already knew this or that this

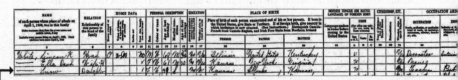

Snow White with her parents in Selma, Fresno County, California, in 1930. *(courtesy of Ancestry.com)*

was new information to me. If it's fresh information, I've just added another generation!

Snow's age is unclear. Perhaps it's thirty-one or thirty-nine. That means I'll have to be flexible as I trace back in time, but it appears she was born in the 1890s in Kansas. And apparently Snow White was a teacher. Assuming she was still working as a teacher in 1937 when the Disney film came out, you have to wonder how her students responded.

Snow White in Selma, Fresno County, California, in 1920. *(courtesy of Ancestry.com)*

Returning to the overall census results, I could easily spot Snow in the 1920 census as she and her parents were in the same place as in 1930—Selma, California. Her age is listed as twenty-seven, which suggests a year of birth of 1892–1893. And here's a little bonus: Snow White had a brother. Although I haven't included the entire page here, it turns out that Snow was already a teacher and her brother Eric was a dentist. If I wanted to learn more about the White family, I could choose at this point to research Eric, but let's stay focused on Snow.

In 1910, the family was already in Fresno County, California, although all the records have consistently listed Snow as having been born in Kansas. Though I haven't mentioned it before, the census records have been giving birthplaces for her parents and their parents as well. From the 1910, we can see that her parents married around 1888 (1910 minus twenty-two years married). Her brother Eric is there and

Snow White in Selma, Fresno County, California, in 1910. *(courtesy of Ancestry .com)*

so is a mystery thirteen-year-old roomer named Mary Warner. If this were my family, I might try to learn more about Mary to determine what the nature of her connection to my relatives was. Based on this record, Snow seems to have been born around 1890–1891, so perhaps she was rounding down her age a touch in later census records—not unusual, especially among women.

Snow White in Eureka, Kansas, in 1900. *(courtesy of Ancestry.com)*

Eureka! In 1900, I finally find Snow White in her native habitat of Eureka, Kansas. The details all match up, with the added insight that she was born in January 1891. Since she was still a child in 1900, there's a good chance this is fairly accurate. If I were to look for a birth record, I would probably start with this date as my first guess. I see also that her parents' marriage took place around 1889 (1900 minus eleven years) and that both of her parents' two children—Snow and Eric—are still living (note the side-by-side columns that say 2 and 2).

Had this been my own family, I would have been saving copies of each of these records, entering the details in my software, perhaps transcribing them into census worksheets (see www.censustools.com for more than 150 free forms), and recording source citations as I went along so it would be easy for me or others to retrace my research trail in the future. If I were using an online tree, I could have "attached" each of these records, so they would be added to each individual's profile and timeline.

At this point, I could keep on marching backward through census records, starting with Snow's father, Simeon R. White, who was consistently listed as having been born in Illinois around 1861–1863. If I look for a circa 1888–1889 marriage record for her parents—most likely in Kansas since her mother was born there—I could probably identify

her mother's maiden name and go backward in time with that branch
as well.

DODGING POTENTIAL PITFALLS

We've just seen how genealogists use census records to work their way
back in time a decade at a time, connecting generations and gathering useful clues that could lead to other records. Generally, it's a fairly
straightforward process, but there can be some hiccups along the way.

Think about how these records were actually recorded—often by
tired and underpaid enumerators going from door to door (perhaps in
crowded tenements or across long distances in remote areas), probably
being less than welcome in some homes, asking slightly nosy questions
of people who could be suspicious, distracted by their seven kids, or
recent arrivals with rudimentary English skills. Compound this with
several opportunities for transcription errors to creep in. Then toss in
ancestors who were missing in action from particular censuses for various reasons (it seems that some of mine are missing from 1870 because
they were attending the funeral of a child in the family, but the flip side
of this is that you can sometimes find ancestors recorded twice in the
same census, as with Helen Keller). Taken together, it's a perfect storm
of circumstances for creating hindrances for the researcher.

All things considered, it's remarkable how easy it is to find most
of our ancestors most of the time. But since forewarned is forearmed,
here's a heads-up of a few of the more common hurdles you might
encounter:

- Poor or old-style handwriting (perhaps with flourishes
  that make it easy to confuse capital letters, etc.).
- Strange or phonetic spellings (for instance, Knight written as Night)—especially when language barriers existed
  or the census taker had limited education.

- Tendency of some of our ancestors (or enumerators) to use nicknames, middle names, or initials.
- People fibbing about or simply not knowing their ages—women were more likely to round down, immigrants were more likely to not know when they were born, and the elderly were more likely to round up (there was a time when being aged gave you bragging rights).
- Varying interpretations of terms such as "mulatto."
- A mishmash of inaccuracies created when worn-out or lazy census takers gathered information from neighbors or others, rather than returning when someone well-informed was home.
- Name changes over time such as those made by immigrants in the decades after arrival or African Americans in the decades following Emancipation.
- Deliberately false entries for political or personal reasons (e.g., padding the numbers in a rural region or attempting to mask polygamy).

You may have noticed a bit of a theme here. The easiest way to conquer the majority of potential obstacles is to be flexible. Those who insist on being very rigid are the ones who will struggle. As long as you accept the reality that some errors and wishful thinking will have crept into your family's records, you'll be in a position to work around them. In fact, the odds are that you'll soon take them for granted and not particularly notice such blips.

CENSUS-WHACKING

I hope what you've just read has left you with a clear understanding of why census records are so incredibly useful for genealogists. Should you, like countless other genies, become enamored of them, I'd like to suggest that you try out a quirky and entirely pointless activity that can nevertheless be an amusing way to spend a little time: census-whacking.

Some of our ancestors had entertaining names. Experience Bliss and Mustard Mustard come immediately to mind, but there are countless others and census records are a great place to find them. When genealogists are in the mood for a break from their usual research, they often go browsing for strange names. I'll leave you with a sampling from The Genealogue, but if you'd like more, you might want to snag a copy of *Bad Baby Names* by Michael Sherrod and Matthew Rayback.

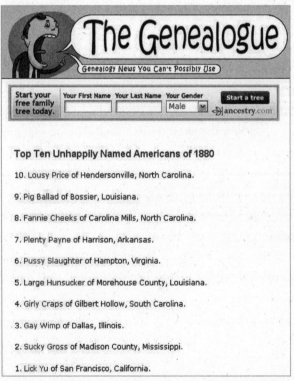

The Genealogue does a little census-whacking in the 1880 census. *(courtesy of Chris Dunham)*

4

VITALLY IMPORTANT: BIRTHS, MARRIAGES, AND DEATHS

Roots sleuths love what are affectionately referred to as BMDs— births, marriages, and deaths. The official versions of these— government-issued birth, marriage, and death certificates—are called vital records, and they truly are vital to your research. There's no better way to prove the links among assorted family members. A birth certificate clearly connects a child to his or her parents and marriage certificates do the same for husbands and wives. Even death certificates frequently include the names of the deceased's spouse and parents. Because of this and the fact that this trio of key events provides a quick outline of an ancestor's life, you'll find yourself turning to them over and over.

But vital records can be challenging to work with. Unlike some countries, the United States does not have centralized registration. These records are mostly held at the state level, but sometimes at the county or even town level, so finding them can take some effort. Compared to many countries, we've been slow to mandate and enforce their filing, with most states not introducing and consistently maintaining them until the last century or so. Then there's the issue of access. Each jurisdiction has its own set of laws pertaining to the public's right to these records—who's entitled and how many years after the event they become open—which tend to shift over time. Cost for a given document can range from free to over fifty dollars (for expedited services), and the content can vary widely depending on the location and time period involved.

Taken on a national level, then, vital records present a patchwork of possibilities and potential problems, but the valuable information they can contain far outweighs the nuisance factor that can be involved. And the good news is that a growing number of state and local governments have joined genealogy Web sites in taking the initiative to place state and county vital records indexes online. Several even offer the certificates—perhaps for a fee, but occasionally free.

WHEN VITALS BEGAN

I hope I'm not dashing anyone's expectations, but in my experience, many new to genealogy have an impression that vital records exist for all the states where their ancestors may have lived all the way back to the time America became America, and maybe even before. We're all so used to this type of paperwork in our own lives that we almost take it as a given that it was part of our ancestors' lives as well. But the reality is that many states didn't start registering vital statistics until the early 1900s—and once they did, there was typically a lag of several years before routine compliance kicked in.

This doesn't mean that you have no chance of finding early vital records. Your odds are best if you have New England roots, as some towns began recording births back in the 1600s, and some of the states themselves did so earlier than most—for example, Massachusetts in 1841, Rhode Island in 1852, and Vermont in 1857. But at the opposite end of the spectrum, there are fifteen states (predominantly southern) that didn't require birth registration until the 1910s. If we were to take the first year of registration for births across all states and average it out, we'd arrive at roughly 1900–1901. The early birds who began before this time? Connecticut, Delaware, Florida, Hawaii (yes, before it was a state), Iowa, Maine, Maryland, Massachusetts, Michigan, New Jersey, New York, Rhode Island, Vermont, and Washington, D.C. Here's hoping that a large proportion of your ancestors spent some time in these states.

THE FUNDAMENTALS OF VITALS

Before exploring the different types of vital records and how to find them, it's worth dwelling on the basics a tad longer. I mentioned that the three types of vital records are birth, marriage, and death records, but it's important to note that the term refers only to documents issued by government offices. It does not include, for instance, baptism, marriage, burial, or other such records maintained by religious institutions. While they often contain overlapping information, vital and religious records (which we'll cover in chapter 7) are considered distinct in the genealogical world. In ideal circumstances, you'll be able to obtain both for an ancestor. This will allow you to confirm certain specifics (such as dates), and it's quite possible that they'll provide complementary information. Perhaps a birth certificate will contain your family's street address, while the corresponding baptism will give the names of your ancestor's godparents. But there are occasions when just one or the other exists, and even times when neither does. Still, it's useful that vital and religious records echo each other because each can serve as an automatic Plan B for the other.

When dealing with vital records, you'll often have the luxury of searching indexes, but this won't always be the case. When indexes don't exist, your best plan of attack is to identify the location and an approximate date. Knowing the location will steer you to the appropriate office or record collection, and having an idea of the date will minimize your digging since many original records are recorded chronologically.

I should also mention that as jarring as this might be to us today, some localities once maintained separate record sets for blacks and whites, so it's worth checking to be sure the appropriate records are searched (in some instances, it could make sense to search both).

In terms of the records themselves, you might wind up with a register entry, a certificate, or a transcription. Many localities—especially those that began recording events fairly early—started with large ledger books in which multiple births, marriages, or deaths were logged on a single page (or often across facing pages). In more recent years, most have used certificates to record a single event in an individual's life. More than likely, for instance, you have a stand-alone birth certificate for your birth. When you request these from the relevant office, you will normally receive a copy (certified or not, according to your request) of the document, but a few (Pennsylvania birth certificates come to mind) provide a transcription instead. This is less desirable as there's always a possibility that the person who processes your request could accidentally inject an error. Fortunately, this situation is the exception to the rule, but to minimize the chances of receiving a transcribed version, it's a good idea to ask for the long form (a full copy) when available.

Finally, because we tend to think in sequential order—birth, then marriage, then death—we'll cover vital records this way, but as with the census, you'll usually find yourself conducting your research in reverse order. Why start with your ancestor's passing? In most states, access to death records is more open than for birth and marriage records (because there are fewer privacy concerns over deceased individuals), so they're easier to obtain. And the majority of us have a better idea of when and where, say, Granddad died than when and where he was born, so we're better equipped to order his death record. You might also have to provide proof of Granddad's death to secure copies of his marriage or birth record since some states restrict access only to the individual himself if still living. For all these reasons, you'll generally seek out an ancestor's vital records in the opposite order in which he experienced these milestone events.

BIRTH RECORDS

Birth records are genealogical gold, but they're also the most restricted of vital records. Because of privacy concerns, many states hold birth records confidential and only give access to documents that are more than one hundred years old—the idea being that researchers can only obtain records for people who are more than likely deceased. This is somewhat frustrating, given that some states haven't even recorded births that long.

But there are exceptions and work-arounds. Some states have shorter limits, such as seventy-five years. Others at least make indexes available, if not the documents themselves. Many states will provide records to researchers if they can prove that the individual in the record is now deceased and that they're the person's next of kin (and of course, you're entitled to a copy of your own birth record). And a few states and localities—much beloved in the genealogical community—place records online once they have aged out of their privacy restrictions (either free or for a fee). We'll see an example of this shortly.

Birth records can be original, amended, or delayed. Most of us have original birth certificates, documents created shortly after birth. An amended one (which is often, but not always, attached to the original) is used to make corrections or other modifications. These are often filed years after the birth when the person in the record discovers an error that must be corrected—say, to apply for Social Security. Delayed records reflect the fact that many states started recording births only during the last century or so. A fellow born in the 1910s who needed a birth certificate for some purpose in the 1950s might discover that he had no official birth record on file. In this case, he would complete the paperwork for a delayed record, often supplying some sort of substantiation of the details of his birth such as a copy of a Bible record (many families used to record births, marriages, and deaths in their family

Bibles, and some still do) or an affidavit from an older relative who recalled his birth. Original and delayed records are filed separately in many states, which is important to know should a search for an original record come up empty. Don't give up, because the record might still exist. Always be sure to look for or ask about delayed records.

What can you learn from a birth record? That depends on the locality and time period involved, but you can usually expect to obtain the following:

- child's name (although early ones sometimes just say "baby" or "girl" or "male")
- date of birth
- place of birth
- gender and race
- father's name
- mother's name (though earlier records might only have the father's and even more recent ones may not include the mother's maiden name)

Beyond this, you might also get some combination of the parents' birthplaces, ages, occupations, and addresses, names of witnesses to the birth (such as doctors and midwives), and the number of children in the family (and sometimes how many are still living).

An example of a typical birth certificate can be seen in the 1927 Arizona birth record for labor leader and civil rights activist Cesar Chavez. Arizona is one of the states that has opted to place records online free of charge (see http://genealogy.az.gov), and that's where the copies on page 85 were found. His record indicates that he was born on March 31, which is now a holiday (Cesar Chavez Day) in eight states. From the original document, we can find many of the details we might hope for—child's name, birthplace and birth date, parents' names, ages, birthplaces, race and occupations, the doctor's name, and the number of children in the family and still living.

Arizona birth certificate for Caesario Chavez (Cesar Chavez) located online. *(courtesy of Arizona Department of Health Services)*

Amendment to Arizona birth certificate for Caesario Chavez (Cesar Chavez) located online. *(courtesy of Arizona Department of Health Services)*

Note also that there's a supplement to this record. The information is essentially the same, but if you look closely, you'll see a few differences—the main one being the spelling of his name. Caesario is now Cesario. There's also a new description of the registration district and the bonus of the father's middle name, a clue to his mother's name. Amendments should always be scrutinized for the clarifications or extra snippets they might furnish. With all this information, you can see why genealogists salivate at the prospect of snagging their ancestors' birth records.

MARRIAGE RECORDS

Marriage records are prized by genies because of their ability to link a husband and wife, and because they're one of the best possible sources for a fiercely sought, but often evasive piece of information—the bride's maiden name. A woman's maiden name is the key to unlocking her pre-Mrs. life and identifying her parents. If you can't discover your great-grandma's maiden name, you're apt to have a stubby branch on your family tree.

When it comes to marriage records, there's good news and not so good news. The upside is that many localities started recording marriages before other vital records, so you may be able to find them for earlier generations of your family. They can also generate a multipart paper trail, which improves your chances of finding at least a portion of it. The downside stems from the fact that marriage records have historically been geographically fragmented. Even today, they're mostly maintained at the county level (except in New York and New England, which function more at a town level).

This dispersion can introduce an extra layer of complexity—not only because each jurisdiction has its own peculiarities, but also because it can force the researcher into a "where'd they marry?" game. When ancestors didn't marry in the expected location, it might be possible to order the record from the relevant state, but the state often requires the requestor to provide the location of the marriage, creating a catch-22. You're hoping to learn the location from the marriage record, but you can't get it if you don't know the location! Some researchers may ultimately end up requesting a marriage record from several government offices—perhaps neighboring counties (or states) or popular wedding destinations—to find the elusive record. Fortunately, many of our ancestors were fairly predictable, marrying where they were born and raised, so you'll probably be able to find most marriage records without much trouble. Just be prepared for that occasional, adventuresome forebear who makes you work a little harder to follow his or her matrimonial trail.

Access to marriage records tends to fall somewhere in between that of birth and death records. To protect the privacy of parties involved who might be alive, a typical restriction is fifty years after the event, although the period varies. During that time, the husband and wife, their next of kin if the couple has passed away, or others with an established legal interest are usually the only ones entitled to the documents. After that, they generally become open records.

When we speak of marriage records, most of us think of certificates, but the nuptial paper trail can also include licenses, registers, affidavits of consent (from parents or guardians of those under the legal age who wish to marry), bonds (guarantees by the groom should the marriage not take place), and banns (a religious tradition of publicly announcing an upcoming marriage so others could share any objections they might have). Although licenses and affidavits are spottier than certificates and registers, they're worth checking for because they can often contain more information. Bonds are more prevalent in certain locations (southern) and banns in certain times (early, such as colonial).

Information contained in marriage records varies, but you can usually expect to find:

- name of the groom
- maiden name of the bride (or perhaps her former married name)
- date of marriage
- place of marriage

With a bit of luck, you might also be rewarded with bride and groom's ages (or possibly their birth dates), addresses, occupations, parents' names (and maybe their birthplaces), the number of previous marriages, and the names and signatures of others involved, such as the official who performed the ceremony (a useful clue for identifying a likely church or religious institution to research for another recording of the marriage) and witnesses.

A typical marriage certificate from New York City shows the type of information that can be gleaned from these records. Virginia O'Hanlon, who wrote the letter that triggered the famous "Yes, Virginia, there is a Santa Claus" response, married Edwin Malcolm Douglas in 1913. Their marriage certificate records Virginia's full name, and includes welcome details such as ages, birthplaces, and parents of the bride and groom. Eagle-eyed readers may notice that one of the witnesses has the same surname as the groom, so was perhaps his sister. This document provides plenty of information, but if this were my family, I might want to retrieve the license from the New York City Municipal Archives to look for additional details. (Incidentally, the Santa Claus letter is in the pos-

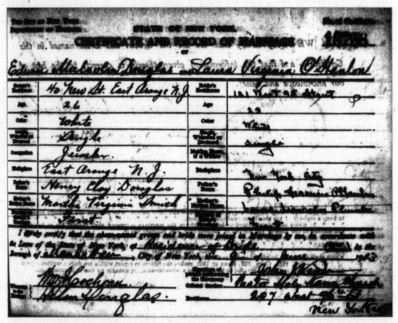

This New York City marriage certificate for the Virginia of "Yes, Virginia, there is a Santa Claus" fame was found on microfilm 1313792 at the Family History Library.

session of Virginia's family and was appraised at roughly fifty thousand dollars on *Antiques Road Show* about a decade ago.)

DEATH RECORDS

Of the three types of vital records, death records are easily the most genie-friendly. Because the subject is obviously deceased, there's less of a concern about privacy, so most states make these records more available. If there's a restricted period, it's usually fairly abbreviated—perhaps twenty or twenty-five years. And death indexes (or even certificates) can be found online, sometimes supplied directly by the states and sometimes by genealogy Web sites.

Another helpful aspect is that many people who were born before births and marriages were regularly registered in their area tend to show up in death records since they're naturally more recent. For instance, an individual born into slavery almost definitely didn't have a birth record, and the prospects of ferreting out a marriage record are iffy at best. But as long as he or she didn't die young, the odds are quite good for finding a death record.

There are also more finding tools for death records. Three of the best include:

- mortality schedules, 1850–1885 (discussed in chapter 3)
- www.deathindexes.com (described in chapter 2)
- Social Security Death Index (SSDI; explained shortly)

Earlier death records are often found in register form, while more recent ones are typically certificates. While you can usually trust basic details such as the date, place, and cause of death, it's smart to evaluate other information carefully. Parents' names and the deceased's birth date and place are notorious for being at least slightly off, if not entirely wrong. If the name of the informant is included, factor that in.

ORIGINAL

MEDICAL CERTIFICATE OF DEATH

STATE FILE NO. 17020

DECEDENT'S BIRTH NO.:

STATE OF ILLINOIS 3-37

DIST. NO. [redacted] 1610

1. PLACE OF DEATH a. COUNTY Cook ILLINOIS

b. CITY (If outside corporate limits, write RURAL and give township or road dist.) OR TOWN CHICAGO

c. LENGTH OF STAY (in this place) 80 YEARS

d. FULL NAME OF HOSPITAL OR INSTITUTION (If not in hospital or institution, give street address or location) 5727 N. Sheridan Rd

2. USUAL RESIDENCE a. STATE ILLINOIS b. COUNTY Cook

c. CITY OR TOWN CHICAGO

d. STREET ADDRESS 5727 N Sheridan Rd

3. NAME OF DECEASED (Type or Print) a. (First) OSCAR b. (Middle) F. c. (Last) MAYER

4. DATE OF DEATH (Month) (Day) (Year) MAR 11 1955

5. SEX MALE

6. COLOR OR RACE WHITE

7. MARRIED, NEVER MARRIED, WIDOWED, DIVORCED (Specify) WIDOWED

8. DATE OF BIRTH MAR 29 1859

9. AGE (In years last birthday) 95

10a. USUAL OCCUPATION MEAT PACKING

10b. KIND OF BUSINESS OR INDUSTRY OWN BUSINESS

11. BIRTHPLACE GERMANY

12. CITIZEN OF WHAT COUNTRY? USA

13. FATHER'S NAME FERDINAND MAYER

14. MOTHER'S MAIDEN NAME MINA WAGNER

15. WAS DECEASED EVER IN U. S. ARMED FORCES? No

16. SOCIAL SECURITY NO. UNKNOWN

17. INFORMANT a. Signature Elsie Mayer Bleuer

b. Address 5727 Sheridan Rd

c. Relationship to deceased daughter

18. CAUSE OF DEATH

I. DISEASE OR CONDITION DIRECTLY LEADING TO DEATH*

Direct cause (a) Arteriosclerotic Heart Disease — Jan 3 - Mar 11 1955

ANTECEDENT CAUSES due to (b) Generalized arteriosclerosis — 15 years

due to (c)

II. OTHER SIGNIFICANT CONDITIONS Bronchial pneumonia — 2 days

19a. DATE OF OPERATION none

19b. MAJOR FINDINGS OF OPERATION

20. AUTOPSY? YES ☐ NO ☒

21a. ACCIDENT SUICIDE HOMICIDE

21b. PLACE OF INJURY

21c. (CITY, TOWN, OR TOWNSHIP) (COUNTY) (STATE)

21d. TIME OF INJURY

21e. INJURY OCCURRED While at work ☐ Not While at Work ☐

21f. HOW DID INJURY OCCUR?

22. I hereby certify that I attended the deceased from March 16 1938 to March 11 1955 that I last saw the deceased alive on March 10 1955 and that death occurred at 2:23 A, from the causes and on the date stated above.

23a. SIGNATURE W. L. Wanier M.D.

23b. ADDRESS AND PHONE NO. 636 Church St. Evanston Ill

23c. DATE SIGNED March 15, 1955

BURIAL (date) MAR. 14 1955

PLACE Cemetery ROSEHILL Location CHICAGO ILLINOIS

RECEIVED FOR FILING ON: 1955 MAR 12 PM 4 54

FUNERAL DIRECTOR Firm Name LAIN & SON INC. Address 5501 N. ASHLAND

Signature F. Theodore Engeln License Number F-3422

LOCAL REGISTRAR Herman N. Bundesen, ILLINOIS

VS&R 280 DEPARTMENT OF PUBLIC HEALTH—Bureau of Statistics

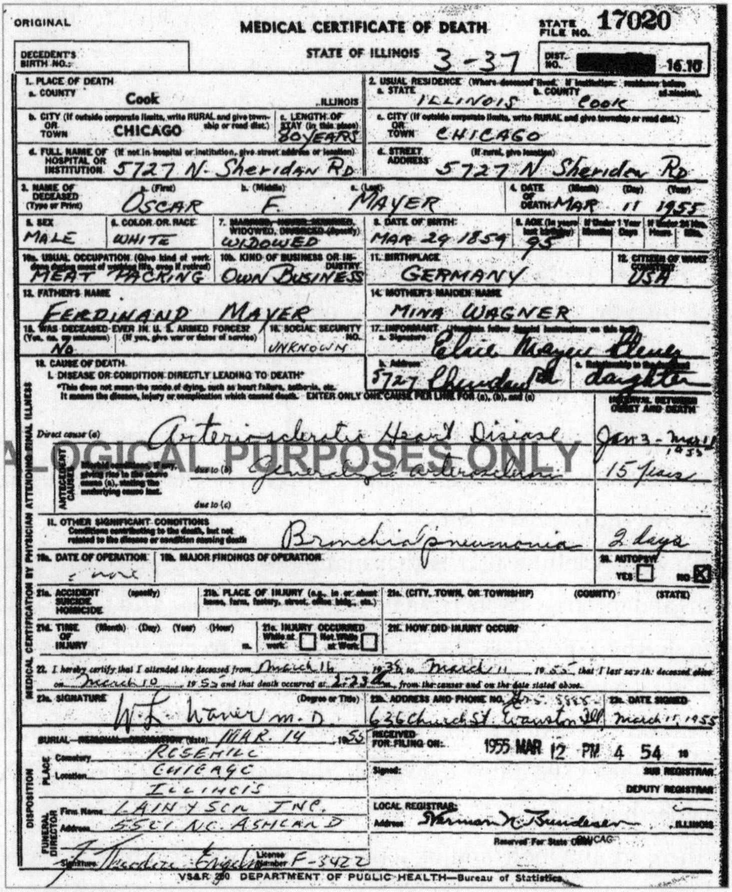

This death certificate for German immigrant Oscar Mayer from the Cook County (Illinois) Clerk's Office Genealogy Online Web site (www.cookcountygenealogy.com) suggests that hot dogs might be good for you. He lived to ninety-five!

A spouse, for instance, is more apt to be accurate about those details than a surviving child.

In most death records, you'll be given the following:

- name of the deceased
- date of death
- location of death
- cause of death
- age at death

You will also frequently find a variety of other details, including the deceased's birthplace and date, last address, occupation, marital status and place of burial, names of the spouse and possibly parents (birthplaces of the parents may be noted, as well as the maiden name of the mother and/or spouse), the name and address of the informant and possibly the physician, and the funeral home that handled the burial. Because of all these potential pieces of information, death certificates are considered to be useful springboard records that can lead you to many other documents, such as cemetery, funeral home, and marriage records, obituaries, and census records for the previous generation.

Some states, such as Texas, have death indexes that can be found online, often on several Web sites. All such indexes, though, can contain errors. The entry for President Lyndon B. Johnson, for example, claims that

Texas Death Index, 1903-2000	about Lyndon Johnson
Name:	**Lyndon Johnson** [Lyndon Baines Johnson]
Death Date:	22 Jan 1973
Death County:	Bexar
Gender:	Male
Marital Status:	Single

The Texas Death Index entry for President Lyndon Baines Johnson lists him as single. *(courtesy of Ancestry.com)*

he was single—an assertion that his wife, Lady Bird Johnson, would probably have challenged. The record itself has recently become available on pilot.FamilySearch.org (try searching yourself), and it's understandable how the transcriber could have made the error: Lady Bird's name is typed vertically along the left edge of the certificate and easy to miss.

SOCIAL SECURITY DEATH INDEX (SSDI)

The Social Security Death Master File (generally referred to as the Social Security Death Index) is a major database of most, but not all, Americans who have died since roughly 1962. There are plenty of exceptions to this. Almost 740,000 who died before 1962 are included and plenty who died afterward aren't (for instance, those who hadn't applied for Social Security or whose deaths weren't reported). Still, packed with more than 85 million names and available free on multiple Web sites, the SSDI is the closest thing the United States has to a nationwide vital records index. A typical SSDI entry includes a person's:

- name
- birth date
- death date (sometimes only the month and year)
- Social Security number (SSN)
- last residence (to the town and zip code level)
- state where the number was issued

While the inclusion of birth dates means the SSDI can help with obtaining birth certificates, most think of it as a valuable finding aid for death certificates. Equipped with the date and location of death from the SSDI, your odds for successfully obtaining a copy of a death certificate increase substantially. Incidentally, while there are occasional calls to remove this database from the Internet because of concerns about its supposed use for identity theft and fraud, it's actually a death verification database used to *prevent* such fraud. Government, financial firms, and other organizations routinely use the SSDI to avoid issuing documents, credit cards, payments, and policies in the name and SSN of deceased individuals.

Links to the database on several Web sites can be found at www .deathindexes.com/ssdi.html, although it exists on still other sites such as FamilySearch.org. Search features vary slightly, so it's worth checking out the different versions to see which appeals to you. All other factors being equal, you may wish to search at Genealogy Bank.com. While this is a subscription-based service, the SSDI is provided free and updated weekly—more frequently than on any other Web site.

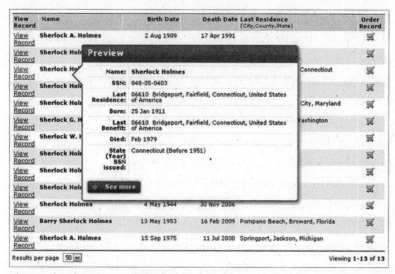

View Record	Name	Birth Date	Death Date	Last Residence (City,County,State)	Order Record
View Record	Sherlock A. Holmes	2 Aug 1909	17 Apr 1991		🛒
View Record	Sherlock Hol				🛒
View Record	Sherlock Ho			Connecticut	🛒
View Record	Sherlock Hol				🛒
View Record	Sherlock Hol			City, Maryland	🛒
View Record	Sherlock G. H			ashington	🛒
View Record	Sherlock W. H				🛒
View Record	Sherlock Hol				🛒
View Record	Sherlock Hol				🛒
View Record	Sherlock Hol				🛒
View Record	Sherlock Holmes	4 May 1944	30 Nov 2006		🛒
View Record	Barry Sherlock Holmes	13 May 1953	16 Feb 2009	Pompano Beach, Broward, Florida	🛒
View Record	Sherlock A. Holmes	15 Sep 1975	11 Jul 2000	Springport, Jackson, Michigan	🛒

Preview

Name:	Sherlock Holmes
SSN:	048-05-0403
Last Residence:	06610 Bridgeport, Fairfield, Connecticut, United States of America
Born:	25 Jan 1911
Last Benefit:	06610 Bridgeport, Fairfield, Connecticut, United States of America
Died:	Feb 1979
State (Year) SSN issued:	Connecticut (Before 1951)

➡ See more

Results per page 50 ▾   Viewing 1-13 of 13

Thirteen gentlemen named Sherlock Holmes have passed away in recent decades. *(courtesy of Ancestry.com)*

If you don't find a person you're searching for, you might want to get creative, as peculiarities and errors can and do slip in. When my mother passed away a few years ago, I wrote an article about the experience of finding her listed in the SSDI for the first time—and how oddly deceptive her entry was. She was recorded by her true first name, a name she disliked and never used, and though married twice, she was listed under her maiden name. Her SSN was issued in a state where our family had lived for only a single year, and as she was a snowbird, the last residence indicated a state other than the expected one. Misspellings, initials instead of names, flip-flopping of numbers—all of these and many other hiccups can be introduced, but a little experimentation will often reveal the person you're seeking.

Information included in the SSDI can also be used to obtain a copy of a (deceased) person's Social Security application (SS-5). Most of the online databases include a link from each entry that generates a letter to the Social Security Administration to request that particular application, but you can also order and pay online (see www.ssa.gov/foia/html/foia_guide.htm). The fee at the moment is twenty-seven dollars, although those not in the index can also be searched for twenty-nine dollars if you can provide details such as place and date of birth. You'll have to be patient as requests typically take three to ten weeks, but the document received is often worth the wait.

In addition to the details in the index, the SS-5 includes full name at birth (a great way to learn women's maiden names), address at the time of application, place of birth, parents' full names (a way to possibly learn maiden names of mothers), employer's name and address, gender, race, date, and signature. While many of these tidbits are also included on the individual's death certificate, the advantage to this document is that the information was supplied directly by that person—not a surviving relative. It's straight from the horse's mouth, so chances are that the parents' names, for example, are accurate on this form even if they're wrong on the death certificate. Though the SS-5 is not a vital record, it's an excellent way to supplement or verify data found in vital records.

OBTAINING VITAL RECORDS

The conventional approach to obtaining copies of vital records is to identify the appropriate government office or archive, follow their request procedure, submit your payment, and wait. The repository you contact will depend on which document you want and the location and the time period you're dealing with, and there are a number of sources to help you find it. Thomas Jay Kemp's *International Vital Records Handbook* is a reliable standard found on the shelves of many libraries and genealogists, and highly recommended.

There are also some online resources you can consult, such as www
.vitalrec.com. Vitalrec.com is a simple Web site organized by state and
counties within each state, and summarizes the availability of birth,
marriage, death, and divorce records, including dates, cost, and links
for ordering. Estimated turnaround times are also sometimes provided.
Costs can occasionally be outdated, so it's a good idea to routinely click
through and browse the Web site of the office you'll be contacting.
Other sources found online are About Genealogy's U.S. vital records
links (http://genealogy.about.com/library/blvitalus.htm) and the Centers for Disease Control and Prevention's page of links to write for vital
records (http://www.cdc.gov/nchs/w2w.htm).

When requesting a record, be sure to follow the process outlined.
Typically, you'll be asked to specify the certificate you want and to furnish the name of your ancestor, along with the approximate date and
location of the event. Some states require additional information such
as the names of the parents for a birth certificate or your relationship
to the person named on the document. It always pays to check out
eligibility requirements so you don't squander time and money making
a request that will be refused.

Many offices offer a genealogical ordering option that provides a
noncertified copy of the record. If you order this way, you can expect to
spend less money, but wait longer. Most offices take a couple of weeks
to a couple of months to respond to genealogical requests, but there are
a few that can take six months or even a year, so review what's online,
ask around or call the office to inquire about turnaround time.

If you're in a hurry, it's also possible to order online via www.vital
chek.com and pay extra to have your request expedited. Documents
requested this way can sometimes arrive overnight (two to five days
is typical), but the shipping and handling fees can be substantial, so
inspect your order carefully before finalizing it. VitalChek also tends to
be stricter that the repositories themselves in terms of its determination
of who is and isn't entitled to a document.

For records that predate statewide registration, you will normally deal with a local office (county or town) or state archive or library. Vitalrec.com will usually point you in the right direction, and most local offices have Web sites that either explain how to order or give a phone number you can call for specifics.

Another option in many cases is the Family History Library (FHL) in Salt Lake City, Utah. Consult the FHL Catalog (presently found under the Library tab on FamilySearch.org—see chapter 2 for more information) for the state or county you're interested in and scroll down to any links for vital records. Alternatively, skim the table on pages 628–631 of *The Source* (available at most libraries and online at www.ancestry .com/wiki) for a tidy summary of what's available. If you find what you're looking for, you can either rent the relevant roll of microfilm (now $5.50 per roll) and have it delivered to your closest Family History Center or hire a researcher in Salt Lake City to pull the record for you. This latter approach is generally more expensive since you'll have to pay for the researcher's time, but can be helpful when time is tight as some will locate a document, scan and e-mail it to you very swiftly. In some instances, I've received documents the same or next day for a price similar to what I would have paid to order directly from the county or state.

IS THERE A SHORTCUT?

Over the last few years, a growing number of vital records indexes—and sometimes even the records themselves—have been placed online. At the moment, this is true of more than thirty states, and especially pronounced with death records, which raise fewer privacy considerations (though some birth and marriage records can also be found on the Internet). Quite a few are provided directly by the state or county, while others can be accessed through FamilySearch or subscriptions to commercial genealogy sites. A surprising number are free, but some cost up to fifteen dollars plus a processing fee. Even when there's a fee involved, though, there's nothing quite like the instant gratification of finding and downloading your great-granddad's death certificate at 2:30 in the morning!

You'll want to seek out online indexes even when you expect to order a certificate the traditional way. If you find one, you'll be able to determine in advance whether the item exists, and the index will frequently give you an exact date (when you might have just had a ballpark guess) and certificate number you can add to your order. This might result in faster service, and also helps avoid frustrating "not found" situations that can occur when, say, a record is not listed under the expected spelling. Researching in person at a state archives, I once discovered the death certificate for one of my great-grandmothers, Mary Reynolds, after receiving one of those dreaded "not found" letters in response to a request I had mailed to the state. She had been recorded as Mary Rynolds, and the missing "e" from her surname was enough to keep her record hidden even though I knew the approximate date of her death. Had I been able to search online and find the certificate number, the record would have been supplied the first time.

How do you find out what exists online? This can be a tad challenging because the terrain is constantly shifting, but I have a handful of Web sites I rely on. I've already mentioned the Social Security Death Index and www.deathindexes.com by Joe Beine, but Joe also offers a companion set of links for online birth and marriage records indexes (go to http://deathindexes.com/sites.html and select Birth, Marriage and Divorce Records).

Another almost accidental resource sports a cumbersome Web address (http://users.rcn.com/timarg/PaHR-Access-states.htm) but is quite handy. A gentleman by the name of Tim Gruber is campaigning to encourage the state of Pennsylvania to relax its unusually restrictive access to death certificates. As part of that initiative, he's created a page with links to others states that have already put older death certificates online—either on their own Web sites or in partnership with one or more genealogical companies or organizations. As of this writing, that includes a dozen—Arizona, Georgia, Kentucky, Massachusetts, Michigan, Missouri, North Carolina, Ohio, South Carolina, Texas, Utah, and West Virginia—with several others reportedly in the process of doing the same. Also included are several localities such as Shelby County, Tennessee, and Philadelphia, Pennsylvania. It's unclear how long this campaign will last, but in the interim, the Web site has become a useful resource for vital records researchers.

I've also made it a habit to routinely scout out indexes and records on:

- Ancestry.com (fee-based for individuals; free at libraries)
- pilot.FamilySearch.org (free)
- Footnote.com (fee-based)
- www.vitalsearch-worldwide.com (fee and free options)
- NewEnglandAncestors.org (dues-based)

All are in the process of adding to their vital records collections, and while there are overlaps, it's not uncommon to find that just one site has the exact year you need. And that's a happy moment indeed when you find just the entry or certificate you're seeking.

VITAL VITALS

Though more challenging to work with than census records, vital records are perhaps the second most useful set of records for genealogists because of their ability to link generations and fill in those basic birth, marriage, and death details for your ancestors. But don't despair if they're not to be found, because there are other options such as religious and cemetery records which will be covered in chapter 7, "The Best of the Rest."

With the twin trends of tightening government budgets and the ever-growing popularity of genealogy, putting indexes and records online is a win-win situation. There have been and will inevitably continue to be sporadic (and sometimes successful) attempts to limit access, but overall, access has been tiptoeing in the direction of openness. And that bodes well for your chances of finding your ancestors' BMDs.

5

MARCHING ORDERS: DID YOUR ANCESTORS SERVE?

For the sake of your family history quest, I hope that you'll discover a number of ancestors who donned a uniform and defended our country. But don't be dismayed if that's not the case, because military records might be useful to you even if your forefathers didn't serve. The World War I draft registration, for instance, was so sweeping that even men born back in late 1872 had to fill out paperwork—and those forms might tell you exactly when and where your great-grandfather was born. They might also toss a surprise at you such as the fact that he had webbed toes or was missing a finger.

And pension files—don't get me started! Every genealogist dreams of finding an ancestor who was denied when he filed for a pension after serving in the Civil War. The harder he (or his widow) had to work to prove entitlement to a monthly stipend, the thicker the resulting paper trail. Your ancestor's battles with bureaucracy can produce a family history bonanza for you (something to keep in mind the next time you're wrestling with the DMV, IRS, or VA).

Naturally, many researching these records do so because they're interested in the military exploits of their forebears. But please don't neglect them if you're the type who's not especially intrigued by this soldiering aspect of their lives. If you do, you'll be missing out, because

military records can be very informative, both in tossing out genealogical tidbits and in rounding out your ancestors as real people.
They're among the most likely to give you a physical description, and
I know of quite a few cases where military files have finally revealed
some long-sought piece of information such as a former slave owner's
name. For those who are captivated by martial history, you may be able
to garner such insights as which battles your ancestors fought in, the
nature of any injuries sustained, where they're buried, and any medals they were awarded. Many who use these records primarily for genealogical purposes often find themselves being lured into the world of
military history because it's now part of their own history. Once you
discover the great-great-grandfather who died at Camp Anderson-
ville, you'll suddenly find yourself hungry for information about this
notorious Civil War prison. It's a slippery slope, so don't say I didn't
warn you.

MILITARY RESEARCH

In general, military records are less centralized than census records,
but less scattered than vital records. Many can be found at two facilities—
the National Archives and Records Administration (NARA) in Washington, D.C., and the National Personnel Records Center (NPRC)
in St. Louis, Missouri—and on two Web sites—Ancestry.com and
Footnote.com.

It's often easier to begin your quest online because Internet-based
resources allow you to search multiple military databases at once,
whereas most on-site research typically requires checking a series of
specialized microfilms. Because of this and the fact that so much has
come online over the last few years, you'll hear repeated references to
Ancestry and Footnote in this chapter, but there are significant record
sets available only at the actual repositories.

There are also certain tried and true records that researchers turn to repeatedly, and the bulk of our collective attention tends to go to World Wars I and II, the Civil War, and the American Revolution (though your ancestors may have also served in a number of other wars—French and Indian, 1812, Mexican-American, Spanish-American, Korean, Vietnam, or Gulf—or perhaps in peacetime).

Most of what follows will focus on these high-interest repositories, Web sites, records, and conflicts. Should you find yourself sliding down that slippery slope into military history obsession, though, there are many additional books, Web sites, and resources you can turn to. While the site is presently heavy on census and vital records, I would suggest keeping an eye on pilot.FamilySearch.org for the addition of military records over time. And I highly recommend *Military Service Records at the National Archives,* which can be downloaded free at www.archives .gov/publications (it's usually at the top of the "most requested items" list). Once you've digested that, there are countless conflict-, regiment-, and location-specific resources awaiting your scrutiny.

WHO SERVED?

Availability of records depends on many factors—which conflicts your ancestors participated in, which branch of the service they belonged to, whether they were officers or not, and so forth—but the first step is identifying those who served. In some cases, you may have heard family stories, seen sepia-toned photos of men in uniform, caught a remark in an obituary, or spotted other clues such as markings on an ancestor's tombstone, but it's worth investigating any male forebear of a likely age to have served in particular American conflicts.

For instance, ancestors born in the 1840s would be prime candidates to have participated in the Civil War. While considering men aged eighteen to thirty or so is a good rule of thumb, it pays to be generous with age ranges. Having conducted extensive research for the U.S. Army, I've worked on cases for a few who managed to enlist underage as recently as the Korean War. Social Security and other record-keeping wasn't as formalized as it is now, so a clever sixteen-year-old was occasionally still able to slip through the cracks—you can imagine, then, what might have been possible during the Revolution or the War of 1812. At the other end of the spectrum, there have been plenty of patriots who understated their age to serve, so don't discount older ancestors without at least a cursory look.

One of my favorite tactics for finding those who served is spot-checking the census records that include some indication of service. We covered this earlier in chapter 3, but here's a quick refresher:

- Revolutionary War pensioners or their widows can be found in the 1840 U.S. Federal Census.
- Civil War veterans or their widows can be found in the 1890 Union Veterans Census.
- Survivors of the Union or Confederate army or navy are noted in the 1910 U.S. Federal Census.
- Veterans of a variety of conflicts are noted in the 1930 U.S. Federal Census.

If you spot an ancestor who served in one of these census records, a quick search at Ancestry.com and Footnote.com (both subscription-based) might be an effective shortcut for you. Both contain numerous military databases, so it's highly possible that you could spot your great-great-great-grandfather's name in, say, War of 1812 Service Records on Ancestry or Revolutionary War Service Records databases on Footnote. The military content of Ancestry and Footnote overlaps, but each has something the other doesn't and you'll occasionally find that one is indexed when the other isn't, so I suggest checking both.

If you have an ancestor in mind and an educated guess about the

Page No. _____
Supervisor's District No. _18_
Enumeration District No. _670_

Eleventh Census of the United States.

SPECIAL SCHEDULE.

SURVIVING SOLDIERS, SAILORS, AND MARINES, AND WIDOWS, ETC.

Persons who served in the Army, Navy, and Marine Corps of the United States during the war of the rebellion (who are survivors), and widows of such persons, in _City of N.Y._, County of _N.Y._, State of _N.Y._, enumerated in June, 1890.

Schuyler De Milt _Enumerator._

House No.	Family No.	Names of Surviving Soldiers, Sailors, and Marines, and Widows.	Rank.	Company.	Name of Regiment or Vessel.	Date of Enlistment.	Date of Discharge.	Length of Service.			
1	2	3	4	5	6	7	8	Yrs.	Mos.	Days	
		De Milt, Henry R.	Corpol	I	22 N.Y. Inf.	3 June 1863	July 1863	0	1	0	1
		Clark, Emmons	Capt	B	7 N.Y. Inf.	19 Apl 1861	3 June 1861	0	5	0	2
		Van Pelt, Gilbert L.	Privat	C	9 N.Y. Inf.	May 1861	Sept 1861	0	4	0	3
		Sandborn, Thomas L.	L'Lieut	D	11 N.Y. Inf.	Sept 1862	Feby 1863	0	6	0	4
		Hill, Sylvester A.	Privat	B	23 N.Y. Inf.	186	186				5
		Julia D. Grant, widow of Ulysses S. Grant	General		U.S. Army	186	186				6
		Marks, David	Brigt		U.S. Army	186	186				7
		Parker, James H.	Priva	K	Conf. Army	186	186				8
		Norris, Alexander H.	Priva		U.S. Army	186	186				9
		Coleman, Michael J.	Privat			186	186				10
		John McCollum	Privat			186	186				11
		Susan De La Montayne, widow — Ole Montayne	Privat			186	186				12

	Post-Office Address.	Disability Incurred.	Remarks.	
	10	11	12	
1	288 Water St. N.Y. City			1
2	59 East 67th N.Y. City		Enlisted & discharged 2 times within this	2
3	123 East 69 St. N.Y. City	Pulmonalis & Inf. Rheumatism		3
4	38 East 70 St. N.Y. City			4
5	37 East 67 St. N.Y. City		Partic away could not learn further	5
6	3 East 66 St. N.Y. City		Further particulars unknown by widow	6
7	51 East 67 St. N.Y. City		Partic away further particulars unknown	7
8	18 East 69 St. N.Y. City		(by family)	8
9	51 East 66 St. N.Y. City		" " "	9
10	38 East 69 St. N.Y. City		Could learn no further particulars	10
11	Baptist Home 68th St. near 4 Ave.		Further particulars unknown by widow	11
12			Reavis person does not... further	12

Julia D. Grant
widow of Ulysses S. Grant   General U.S. Army

Further particulars unknown by widow

These snippets taken from the 1890 Union Veterans Census show that Ulysses S. Grant's widow knew that he was a general in the army, but didn't know "further particulars" of his service. *(courtesy of Ancestry.com)* conflict in which he served, you'll also want to browse Joe Beine's list of online searchable military records and databases (www.military indexes.com). Organized by war and sometimes geographically within a war, this set of links will quickly steer you to the best of what's online, both free and fee-based. Examples of conflict-specific resources included are the popular Civil War Soldiers and Sailors database (www.itd.nps .gov/cwss, free) and the American Civil War Research database (www .civilwardata.com, fee-based). Be sure to scroll down to the bottom where he's placed some useful general resources that aren't restricted to a single conflict. Another more detailed list also worth consulting is Cyndi Howells's military links (www.cyndislist.com/military.htm). I often start with Joe's list and later visit Cyndi's to find those hidden gems, such as a Web site dedicated to the regiment or battle an ancestor served in.

TYPES OF RECORDS

An individual ancestor may show up in several different types of military records, so it helps to have a basic understanding. Through the course of his military career, he would have been drafted or enlisted, then served, and possibly have received some postservice compensation such as a pension or bounty land. Each of these would have created a paper trail, although not all will necessarily still survive. Depending on the circumstances, he might have left more traces ranging from state-awarded medals to discharge papers at a county courthouse, but we'll start with the basic hire-to-retire cycle.

Enlistment and Draft Registration

It wasn't all that long ago that enlistment and draft registration documents were fairly low on genealogists' wish lists, but now they're among some of the most popular. This is mainly due to increasing accessibility. Some used to be available only through on-site research at NARA (mostly in Washington, D.C., and at the NARA's Southeast Region facility in Georgia) and others only recently aged out of privacy restrictions. But now, millions have been scanned, indexed, and placed online at Ancestry.com or transcribed and made searchable on the main NARA Web site (http://aad.archives.gov/aad).

Another factor driving their popularity is sheer volume. So many of our ancestors made an appearance in World War I or II records (and sometimes both) that your chances of netting a few are very good. Genealogically speaking, these records are quite contemporary, so they're often among the first that new genies use since we usually start with ourselves and go backward in time. Many will find some combination of themselves, their fathers, their grandfathers, and their great-grandfathers in these records.

World War II Army Enlistment Records

World War II Army Enlistment Records (1938–1946) can be found on both the NARA and Ancestry.com Web sites. While this database doesn't contain information on everyone who served in the Army during World War II, approximately 8.4 million men and women are included. Yes, you read correctly. I said *women*. Many who served in the Women's Army Auxiliary Corps can be found here. In fact, if you're the kind who likes to play with databases, you can quickly discover almost 7,800 by the name of Mary who enlisted.

Details you can hope to find are name, serial number, residence (county and state), place of enlistment, enlistment date, Army branch and grade, term of enlistment, year and state of birth, race and citizenship, education, marital status, and sometimes height and weight.

World War II Draft Registration Cards

Only a fraction of the World War II draft registration cards that exist are open to the public, but that translates into more than seven million cards on Ancestry.com alone. Others are available through the

U.S. World War II Army Enlistment Records, 1938-1946 about Hugh M Hefner

Name:	**Hugh M Hefner**
Birth Year:	1926
Race:	White, citizen *(White)*
Nativity State or Country:	Illinois
State of Residence:	Illinois
County or City:	Cook
Enlistment Date:	12 Jun 1944
Enlistment State:	Illinois
Enlistment City:	Fort Sheridan
Branch:	No branch assignment
Branch Code:	No branch assignment
Grade:	Private
Grade Code:	Private
Term of Enlistment:	Enlistment for the duration of the War or other emergency, plus six months, subject to the discretion of the President or otherwise according to law
Component:	Reserves - exclusive of Regular Army Reserve and Officers of the Officers Reserve Corps on active duty under the Thomason Act (Officers and Enlisted Men -- O.R.C. and E.R.C., and Nurses-Reserve Status)
Source:	Enlisted Reserve or Medical Administrative Corps (MAC) Officer
Education:	4 years of high school
Marital Status:	Single, without dependents
Height:	61
Weight:	166

Hugh Hefner's World War II army enlistment. *(courtesy of Ancestry.com)*

National Archives and its regional branches, as well as the Family History Library in Salt Lake City. Still more that are presently covered by privacy laws will become available over time.

The ones that are already accessible are from the fourth registration, often referred to as the "old man's draft." The Selective Service Act introduced when the United States entered World War II was so encompassing that all men between the ages of eighteen and sixty-five had to register. Registration was accomplished in waves, with the fourth one being directed at older men (not already in the military) born between April 28, 1877, and February 16, 1897—those ages forty-five and up.

Some or all of Arkansas, California, Connecticut, Delaware, Illinois, Indiana, Maryland, Massachusetts, New Hampshire, New Jersey, New York, Ohio, Pennsylvania, Puerto Rico, Rhode Island, Vermont, Virginia, and West Virginia are searchable on Ancestry.com. If you find an ancestor, you'll get their age, birth date and place, residence, employer details, physical description (sometimes including remarks about lost digits and limbs and other physical factors that could affect one's ability to serve), and the name and address of a person who would always know how to reach the registrant. This last detail can provide an important clue. While it's often the registrant's wife, it sometimes lets you know of a sibling or child, possibly living in another town or state. I've found this to be especially helpful with immigrants who were bachelors or outlived their spouses, as this piece of information can lead to other immigrants from the same family.

Regrettably, original cards for eight states (Alabama, Florida, Georgia, Kentucky, Mississippi, North Carolina, South Carolina, and Tennessee) were destroyed before they were microfilmed, so those records are lost. But many men originally from these states migrated north before 1942, so they can be found in the cards for other states. In fact, I'm often struck by how this particular collection captures at least a part of the African American migration to the north and west.

World War I Draft Registration Cards

This collection is a genealogist's dream. While it was less comprehensive age-wise than the World War II draft, for World War I all men (not already in the military) between eighteen and forty-five were supposed to register. All told, some 24 million men did. That's about half the men living in America at the time, so it's a rare family indeed that doesn't find a few of its male ancestors in the mix.

This registration was conducted in three waves and different cards were used, so the data gathered varies. In general, you can expect to learn your ancestor's full name, address, place and date of birth, race and country of citizenship, occupation and employer, and physical description. You'll also get to see his signature and may get other particulars such as the name of the closest relatives, marital status, or father's birthplace.

One of the reasons these cards are so popular with genealogists is that they provide an alternative for discovering birth dates and places for ancestors born before vital records were routinely maintained in most states. And many a researcher has finally learned what town their immigrant great-granddad came from in Russia or Italy from his World War I draft registration card. The fact that a quarter of America's population at the time is included only enhances this collection's value.

The originals of these records are located at the National Archives Southeast Region in Georgia (and can be ordered from http://friend snas.org; click on "Finding Aids" and then "WWI Draft Request"). Other regional branches of NARA and some major libraries hold records for their state or region, while the Family History Library in Utah also houses an extensive collection. But the easiest way to search is on Ancestry.com (either through a paid membership or free at a library). See www.genealogybranches.com/worldwaronedraftcards .html for more information.

REGISTRATION CARD

Al Capone gave his occupation as paper cutter on his World War I draft registration card. *(courtesy of Ancestry.com)*

Incidentally, if you enjoyed census-whacking, you might also enjoy browsing for some of the famous men found in the World War I draft, but there's no need to research them yourself. NARA's Southeast Region has already done that for you (www.archives.gov/southeast/wwi-draft) with links to everyone from Fred Astaire to Babe Ruth.

U.S. Army Register of Enlistments, 1798–1914

I consider this set of records to be one of the better kept secrets in genealogy. Originals are retained at the National Archives, but a digitized
and searchable database is also available on Ancestry.com (you can go
directly to this database by clicking "search all records" at the top of
the page, selecting "Military" and scrolling down to "U.S Army Register of Enlistments"). I suspect it slips beneath the radar because it's not
associated with a particular conflict, but many of our ancestors made a
career of the Army.

These records are in register form with one individual per line, usually on a pair of facing pages. That may not sound like much, but that
single entry can reveal your ancestor's age, birthplace, date and place of
enlistment, occupation, physical description, rank, company and regiment, and date and cause of discharge. For immigrants who arrived
in the late 1700s through the mid-1800s or so, it might just divulge
the town or region in his country of birth. And remarks appended
at the far right can often be enlightening. Notes about injury ("accidentally shot in foot") and character ("good when sober") are quite
common.

It's fortunate that many reenlisted, so you may be lucky enough to
find a regular entry for your ancestor every five years until he left the
service for the last time. Another similar database is the U.S. Marine
Corps Muster Rolls (1798–1940). These muster rolls (frequent lists of
those in a military unit) often contain enlistment details. Curious about
Michael Strank, one of those who raised the flag at Iwo Jima, I searched
for him and found seventeen entries in 1939 and 1940, as well as the
fact that he enlisted on October 6, 1939. Both of these databases are
also useful for chasing collateral lines, so if you don't find your direct
line ancestor, take a few more minutes to search for his brothers, uncles,
and cousins.

Personnel Records and Compiled Service Records

Once your ancestors actually enter the military, a fresh paper trail recording their service is set in motion. Most of these records are held either at the National Archives and Records Administration in Washington, D.C., or at the National Personnel Records Center in St. Louis, Missouri. In general, those from World War I and later are in St. Louis, while the older ones are in Washington. Their availability depends on time period, branch of service, and a few fires (more on this shortly), and somewhat counterintuitively, the older ones are often easier to obtain.

Personnel Records

NPRC in St. Louis is the repository for the bulk of twentieth-century personnel records for the Army, Navy, Air Force, Marine Corps, and Coast Guard, but a fire in 1973 consumed a large portion of these records. Files for approximately 80 percent of those discharged from the Army between November 1, 1912, and January 1, 1960, and roughly 75 percent of those with surnames from Hubbard through "Z" discharged from the Air Force between September 25, 1947, and January 1, 1964, were destroyed. Records for the Navy, Marine Corps, and Coast Guard fared better.

While this is unfortunate, it doesn't mean that you shouldn't try for these records. Even if the main portion of your ancestor's file burned, you may still be able to obtain bits and pieces such as medical and dental records. Also, yours might be among those that survived. I once saw a file that was singed along the edges but otherwise intact. It's always worth checking.

Unlike most of the other military records we've discussed until now, these personnel files cannot be found online. If you are the next of kin of a deceased veteran, you can write to NPRC to request his or her file (go to www.archives.gov/st-louis/military-personnel/index.html for links and instructions). Those who are not next of kin will need to use Standard Form 180 found on the same page. NPRC processes thousands of requests each week, and genealogical inquiries that require reconstruction as a result of the fire take longer than most, but things are improving. What used to take a year or so is now measured in months. You can also visit St. Louis in person or hire a researcher, but in my experience, even on-site research requires at least two visits. If you are in a hurry, though, hiring a local professional may expedite the procedure.

Compiled Service Records

In 1800 and 1814 another pair of fires destroyed many Army and Navy records. This coupled with the deteriorating condition of many other records prompted the War Department to begin an initiative a little over a century ago to gather information for individual soldiers. Packets of index cards with details abstracted from muster rolls, enlistment and discharge records, payrolls, hospital records, prison records, and other sources were created for each soldier. This packet is referred to as a Compiled Service Record.

Found mainly for those who served in the Revolution, War of 1812, and Civil War, these records are available at the National Archives in Washington, D.C., but have started to appear online in recent years. Footnote.com, for instance, has Compiled Service Records for the Revolutionary War and a portion of those for the Civil War. Whether your ancestor's is on the Internet will depend on where and when he served. If you don't find him now, you can order his file directly from NARA (go to www.archives.gov/research/order), hire a researcher in Washington, D.C., or wait a few months and search online again. At the current pace of digitization, you might not have to wait long to surf your way to the records you seek.

Compiled Service Records typically provide a brief outline of your ancestor's military career, but tend to be light on other details. They're a terrific resource for walking in your forefather's military footsteps, perhaps even on the very battlefields in which he fought. But those hoping for genealogical data will often use them as a stepping-stone to files with more personal information, such as pensions.

Pension Files and Bounty Land Warrants

Pension and bounty records admittedly sound about as exciting as dirt, but ask any genealogist about their experience with Civil War pensions and prepare yourself for a breathless recounting of some breakthrough discovery. Bounty land records aren't always quite as thrilling, but you'd be surprised at the family history tidbits they can contain. Both were forms of inducement or reward for military service and created a paper trail much appreciated by genies today.

Pension Records

Always check for pension files for ancestors who served in the Civil War or Revolutionary War. Always! These apply mostly to those who served in the 1800s or slightly before or after. The majority were filed by the soldier himself or his widow, but you'll occasionally find them filed on behalf of orphans and other heirs.

Pensions were intended to provide a stipend to assist those who were sick or incapacitated as a result of their service, as well as the elderly or survivors of a deceased veteran who relied on him for their support. That might leave you with the impression that the records will be nothing but medical documents, but that's usually not the case. More often than not, they're much more.

Even if your ancestor's file is fairly bare-bones, you're apt to learn more about him as a person. You may get his own account of the battles he served in or the wounds he sustained. If he could write, you'll get his signature. If he was married and had a family, you'll get substantiation of that—perhaps dates and places for his marriage and the births of his children. Parents' names and wives' maiden names are frequently

George Armstrong Custer's widow applied for a pension after losing her husband
at Little Bighorn. *(courtesy of Footnote.com)*

included, birthplaces in the old country may be found, and names of
former slave owners (for the veteran himself and maybe his wife) might
be provided. You might even find torn-out pages from the family Bible
sent in as proof of some family details.

When it comes to pension files, red tape is a good thing. Your ancestor's tussles with bureaucracy could translate into a thick file for you to
explore today. If his or his widow's claim was rejected, you'll often find
a stash of affidavits, primarily from people backing the claim. These
might be from soldiers who served with him, neighbors vouching for
his good health before he joined the military, or relatives backing the
widow's assertion of having been the legal and only wife of the soldier. For that matter, I suggest you make a habit of looking into those
who testified in one way or another for the soldier because they were

frequently relatives of some sort. Brothers-in-law, for instance, are heavily represented so I've found this to be a handy means of backing into the married names of soldiers' sisters.

By the way, don't be surprised to find a whiff of scandal. Over the years, I've encountered quite a few files for soldiers with more than one purported widow. You'll also sometimes find cross-pollinated files from two men claiming to be the same soldier. Or you might find your ancestor's claim rejected because the government is convinced that he's already dead! In general, the more complicated the situation, the better for you. Confusion begets paperwork, and you'll have a lot more to scrutinize.

Not surprisingly, Civil War pension files are generally riper with genealogical detail than those from the Revolutionary War, but even these earlier ones can be family treasures. You might finally find proof of your patriot's marriage back in the late 1700s or early 1800s or be able to read in his own words how proud he was to be an eyewitness to the surrender of Cornwallis at Yorktown.

Pension indexes can be found online at Ancestry.com and Footnote .com. See www.militaryindexes.com for direct links for the conflict that interests you. Nonfederal pensions, such as those granted by states to men who served in the Confederacy, are retained at the state level, frequently in state archives and libraries. This Web site will point you to many of these lesser known, specialized resources as well. Incidentally, if your Confederate ancestor served in one state, but moved to another, he would have filed from the state he settled in.

Using the details provided in the indexes, you can obtain copies of your ancestor's records from the National Archives, which holds all that were federally issued. Digitized pensions for the Revolutionary War and a small portion of widows' pensions from the Civil War can also be found online at Footnote.com. Searching is free, but you'll have to subscribe to view the documents.

At present, the only way to obtain most Civil War pension files

This excerpt from the Revolutionary War pension file for African American patriot Agrippa Hull details his 1813 marriage to Margaret Timbroke and demonstrates that older records can take some patience and squinting to read! *(courtesy of Footnote.com)*

is by ordering them from NARA (www.archives.gov/research/order/ orderonline.html), going there yourself, or hiring a researcher. These files can be extensive and awkward, with papers of all sizes and writing on both sides, so it takes some effort to copy one. Accordingly, the cost for ordering a full file from NARA is comparatively steep (presently seventy-five dollars for the first one hundred pages plus sixty-five cents per additional page), so you might find it cost effective to find a researcher to copy the file for you.

These incredible records weren't microfilmed, so you're actually given the original documents when you research on-site. While it's an amazing experience to hold a letter your ancestor wrote, it's also a little intimidating because they're often in delicate condition. The good news in terms of preservation is that this tremendous set of records is now being scanned. As just mentioned, a small sample is available now at Footnote, but more intensive digitalization efforts are under way, so we can all look forward to easier online access within the next few years.

Bounty Land Warrants

Starting in 1776, the federal government offered bounty land in return for military service. In addition to functioning as a form of compensation, it was hoped that offering this free land would entice former soldiers to help settle and protect the frontier. This scheme was in place until 1855, so ancestors who served in the Revolutionary War, War of 1812, Indian Wars before 1855, or the Mexican War are most likely to have applied.

Eligible soldiers would complete a bounty land warrant application, usually at their local courthouse. Assuming they were approved, they would receive a warrant which could then be used to apply for a land patent. It was the patent that actually transferred ownership of the land to the veteran, but before restrictions were implemented, many sold their warrants.

Generally speaking, the later the application, the better the odds that a file exists and will include a prize or two like marriage, death, and Bible records. Some of the early portion of this paper trail was destroyed in the 1800 and 1814 fires mentioned previously, so surviving records from the Revolutionary War were combined with pension files. All of these records are housed at the National Archives and can be ordered directly or using the services of a researcher, as with pension files. Bounty land applications from the Revolutionary War can also be found on Footnote, and some states such as Virginia offered their own bounty land programs. Check the state archives or www.militaryindexes.com for links to point you in the right direction.

Other Military Resources

While we've covered the major places your military ancestors may have
left traces, it's not possible to cover them all, so I'd like to leave you with
a menu of other possibilities to explore. With most of what follows, if
you can't easily find what you're looking for, a few minutes spent browsing MilitaryIndexes.com and the military section of Cyndi's List (www
.cyndislist.com/military.htm) would probably be time well spent.

Casualty and Remembrance Lists
A number of official (and some nonofficial) lists of those who lost their
lives, were injured, or went missing in action are found on Ancestry
.com, Footnote.com, and a variety of other Web sites. Some allow you
to post remembrances as a way to honor those who served. A few I visit
often are:

- National World War II Memorial (www.wwiimemorial
  .com)
- Korean War Project (http://koreanwar.org)
- Vietnam Veterans Memorial (http://thewall-usa.com)

Medal Recipients
These range from Medal of Honor citations (www.history.army.mil/
moh.html) to state-specific collections. I was delighted recently to find
the paperwork associated with a medal awarded to an Italian immigrant grandfather of my husband's for his service in World War I. In
this case, it was the Pennsylvania state archives that offered the collection online (www.digitalarchives.state.pa.us/archive.asp).

Discharge Papers
Those in your family who served in World War I or II will likely have
filed discharge papers at their local county courthouse. A few earlier

ones may also exist. For the most part, these are held in the counties where they were filed, but copies of some can be found at the Family History Library. These papers typically provide a brief overview of an individual's military service, so can serve as a partial substitute for those whose personnel records were destroyed in the 1973 fire at NPRC.

Regimental Histories

When military buffs speak of regimental histories, they're usually referring to the Civil War. Reading unit histories is one of the best ways to fully appreciate what your ancestor experienced and endured. Two of the best resources for tracking down relevant ones are the Library of Congress (www.loc.gov/rr/main/uscivilwar) and the Civil War Archive (www.civilwararchive.com/regim.htm).

Societies

I hope for your sake that you're not the first descendant of a soldier who served in the Revolutionary War to discover his contributions. Assuming you're not, you may well be able to tap into applications filed by assorted relatives attempting to join a military lineage society. Some of the better known include Daughters of the American Revolution (www.dar.org/library) and Sons of the American Revolution (www.sar.org), but other wars also spawned societies you may wish to research or join, such as the General Society of the War of 1812 (www.societyofthewarof1812.org).

State Archives

State archives and libraries are an underappreciated resource for those conducting military research. It may take a little more digging to see what they have to offer (visit www.statearchivists.org/states.htm for links or simply Google "state archives" and the state you're interested in), but you never know what you might find. New Jersey, for instance, offers indexes to Civil War vouchers and claims for Revolutionary War damages. Other states provide digitized images online such as Florida Confederate pension application files or World War II correspondence involving residents of Alabama. Not long ago, I found myself captivated reading letters written by a Red Cross volunteer sitting in a posh residence in Germany that had recently been seized from the Nazis.

Local and Family Resources

True, they're the hardest to track down and dig through, but collections held in local libraries, genealogical and historical societies—or by the scattered branches of your own family—can yield genealogical treasures. My sleuthing was rewarded once with a photo of my maternal grandfather while he served in World War I. Also included was the transcription of a letter he had written home. Where did I find it? In a newsletter for the employees of the company he worked for before going overseas. One of my distant cousins had it, but I might have

CORPORAL JAMES V. SHIELDS
Co. C, 104th Field Signal Battalion

Just in the rear of the third-line trench. While on our way we took a rest by the roadside. We were not there but three minutes when the guns from our side of the line began to try to find the range of the big German gun that has been doing so much damage. This was the first gun. We were so near it was only about 100 yards from us and hidden in the woods. As soon as the first shot was fired we all jumped to our feet and started off again, because we knew the German guns would begin. We had gone only about fifty yards when one shell went flying over our heads and landed about 100 yards from us. Did we walk faster? I should say so.

I particularly enjoy the last few lines of this letter my grandfather wrote in a letter home from World War I. (courtesy of author)

also found it in the local library. RootsWeb county sites are a good place to try to learn about these local repositories.

FORWARD MARCH!

Though it was far from their original intent, military records are a treasure trove for genealogists. The paper trail your patriotic ancestors left can sometimes tell you more about their lives than all other sources combined, so they're always worth exploring even if you've never heard so much as a whisper of military service in your family. And while I don't wish to be unkind to your predecessors, my hope for you is a handful of ancestors whose pension claims were initially denied, creating stacks of paper for you to peruse.

6

CROSSING THE POND:
OLD COUNTRY ROOTS

Unless you're of pure Native American ancestry, you have roots in at least one other continent. The only question is how far into your search you'll encounter a foreign-born ancestor. Once you do, the natural tendency is to want to follow the trail overseas to see where it leads. Before you book a flight for Germany or China, though, you'll want to do a little more digging on this side of the ocean.

If you have notions of visiting your ancestral homeland, walking in your immigrant ancestor's footsteps, or meeting people who look strangely like you but speak another language, identifying the exact city, town, or village your ancestor first called home is the key to unlocking your old country past. This can be challenging to discover, but there are plenty of records and resources in America that might hold this vital clue. In this chapter, we'll talk about tactics for finding this critical piece of information and what to do once you discover it.

IMMIGRATION RESEARCH

While there are a variety of records that can help you cross the pond, the ones genealogists turn to most often are passenger arrival and naturalization records, so we'll start with them. The availability of records for your ancestors will depend on several factors such as their port of arrival and whether they bothered to get naturalized, but the overriding determinant is the time period. In general, the more recently your forebears came to America's shores, the better the paper trail. Those who came through Ellis Island, for instance, will be much easier to trace than those who arrived in colonial times. And the documentation you locate will usually be more revealing for more recent immigrants.

Fortunately, passenger lists are fairly centralized and found mainly at the National Archives. NARA's immigration records are also available through the Family History Library, and other larger or genealogically focused libraries (such as Allen County Public Library in Fort Wayne, Indiana) around the country often offer a sizable collection. Naturalization records are more dispersed and might be located at the National Archives, U.S. Citizenship and Immigration Services, or local courthouses. The Family History Library also has some of the naturalization records found at NARA and selected courthouses.

In terms of online resources, Ancestry.com provides an impressive collection that combines arrival and naturalization records, making it easy to search for your ancestors regardless of when they came and whether they arrived at New York, Seattle, or New Orleans. At present other Web sites are lighter on such records, but Footnote.com has some naturalizations and pilot.FamilySearch.org includes Ellis Island arrivals for 1892–1924. Both will presumably add to these collections over time. You can also search several specialized sites such as EllisIsland .org, and as with other genealogical topics, both Joe Beine and Cyndi Howells offer many useful links on their Web sites. Joe's provides a broad overview (www.deathindexes.com/sites.html), while Cyndi's includes just about every immigration or naturalization link you could possibly imagine (www.cyndislist.com/immigrat.htm).

PRACTICE FLEXIBILITY

I stated at the outset of this book that it's important to be open-minded when it comes to your family's names, and that's particularly true of immigration-related papers. They're more likely than others to toss surprises at you, so please don't lock yourself into a particular spelling. Similarly, families' arrival sagas seem a touch more prone to exaggeration or error than others, so if you're convinced that your ancestor arrived at Ellis Island because Grandma told you so, but don't find him, consider checking other ports such as Philadelphia and Baltimore.

Those from certain areas such as Eastern Europe should also anticipate a little confusion about old country origins. You may have heard the old joke about Great-Granddad having lived in three countries without ever leaving the house he was born in because of constantly changing political and national boundaries. So don't be surprised to find a potpourri of countries recorded for a single ancestor. If this happens to you, just continue to focus your efforts on identifying your ancestor's hometown since that's the most important piece of information.

There's one other way that gentle distortion sometimes slips into immigration records, and the source is usually the immigrant. Many of our ancestors came from tiny villages, towns, or shtetls, but figured that no one here would have ever heard of them, so it's not unusual for them to use the closest large town or city as a proxy. Instead of saying Barwinek, for example, they might say Kraków. That's unfortunate because the records you need to prove your connection to the old country—perhaps religious or census—are probably associated with Barwinek. Worse yet, Barwinek might have one church or synagogue to research, whereas Kraków could have dozens. If your ancestor mentions a small town you have to scrutinize maps to locate, it's probably his true place of origin. But if he mentions a large city, it's not a bad idea

to double-check. Seek additional records of his for verification or perhaps records for collateral relatives—siblings, parents, or cousins who
also emigrated to America. In most cases, at least one document or person will have given the tiny town you're truly interested in, and that will
ultimately save you lots of time.

WHO IMMIGRATED?

The first step in making the leap to the motherland is figuring out who
in your family made the journey to America. Most of us will have multiple immigrants in our family tree, and the longer your family has
been here, the more you'll have. I suggest starting with the most recent
arrivals and working your way back to earlier ones as you gain experience with immigration research. If you happen upon a relatively recent
immigrant who stubbornly hides from view, tackle the others first and
return to him later once you've had a little more practice.

It may be that your family arrived within the last generation
or two, in which case your easiest path is to simply talk with your
elders. At around three to four generations removed from the old country, though, memories start to fade. It's not unusual for Americans to be
unable to name the hometowns of immigrant grandparents, and very
few nongenealogists could name the towns that any of their immigrant
great-grandparents once called home. In fact, many would struggle to
specify even a country.

Once you get past the point of memory, census records offer the easiest way to identify immigrants for the simple reason that those from
1850 on give a place of birth, and those from 1880 on give birthplaces
for each person's parents as well. In most cases, only the country is
listed, but there are happy exceptions. In the 1860 census, for instance,
you may find the region or province in addition to the country, and
more recent census records will often specify whether Irish immigrants

were from the Republic of Ireland or Northern Ireland. Every once in a while, you might even be lucky enough to find a golden hint like "Minsk" written in for your ancestor's birthplace.

As mentioned in chapter 3, those whose immigrant ancestors made an appearance in census records from 1900 to 1930—and given the massive wave of immigration that took place around the last turn of the century, that's a significant percentage of us—can get a running start, since data collected during this period included the year of immigration and hints about naturalization. In the 1920 census, our ancestors were asked the year of their naturalization, but even in the other years the census shows whether they were naturalized (na), alien (al), or had applied for papers (pa). It's quite common to see Grandpa listed as an alien in one census, having applied for papers by the next, and naturalized by the following one.

These date cues are invaluable for leading you to passenger arrival and naturalization records. No matter how uncommon your surname might be in America, chances are that more than one person with your ancestor's name immigrated here, so it's helpful to know that you're looking for the one who came around 1902 as opposed to the one who arrived around 1891. Also, many naturalization records are arranged chronologically, so having a rough date in mind can save you time. My Smolenyak great-grandfather arrived in 1890, but didn't apply for naturalization until 1917 (many who had been here quite a while suddenly scrambled to get their citizenship to demonstrate their loyalty when the United States entered World War I). Learning from the 1920 census that he had applied for papers since the last census told me to concentrate on the 1910s, rather than start my search back in the 1890s.

The farther back in time you go, the harder it becomes to pick up easy clues identifying the immigrant. But the flip side of this is that those who have been in America for more than, say, 150 years were mostly from a handful of countries (the British Isles and Germany being most prevalent) and often have so many descendants living today that it's almost inevitable others will have tackled this same research challenge. These early arrivals were also fewer in number so they can sometimes be found in published sources. For these reasons, your path of least resistance may be to join forces with others who are researching the same people or to consult likely books, CDs, and databases (more on this shortly). If you're one of the lucky ones, you may find a distant cousin who's already solved the immigration riddle for you.

Anything you can learn to narrow your focus will improve your chances of walking in your ancestors' old country footsteps. While it's imperative to identify the immigrant himself, you should also aim for his rough year of immigration and approximate year of birth. This combination of information will best equip you for a successful search in passenger arrival and naturalization records.

IMMIGRATION RECORDS

Passenger arrival records (often called manifests) are typically broken into three broad time periods: pre-1820, 1820–1890, and 1891–1957. Many Americans will have immigrant ancestors sprinkled across all three.

Pre-1820

Pre-1820 or colonial records are random and sparse, primarily because there was no central administration at the time. Initially, the colonies were British and most arriving here—by choice or otherwise—were British subjects or slaves, so there was minimal interest in recording the flow of people. The major exception to this was Germans arriving in Pennsylvania, who had to swear an oath of allegiance starting in 1727. This actually applied to all who weren't British, but in practical terms, that translated to German and Swiss immigrants at the time.

In spite of this spotty record-keeping, names of more than two million early arrivals have been gathered together in a number of published sources, many of which can be found on a list compiled by Joe Beine (www.germanroots.com/1820.html). Those with access to Ancestry .com will also find many of these early lists included in the Immigration & Emigration Records Collection, and though it includes few names, one of the best resources for learning about the forced immigration of slaves is the Trans-Atlantic Slave Trade Database (www .slavevoyages.org).

1820–1890

Due to an act of Congress in 1819, passengers started being more consistently recorded from 1820. The information collected wasn't much—usually just the name of the ship and captain, the port of departure, the date and port of arrival, and passengers' names, ages, genders, occupation (frequently given as laborer), and nationality. But the odds of finding your ancestors in these records escalate at this point. These records, kept by U.S. Customs, are generally referred to as Customs lists and can be found at the National Archives, through the Family History Library and its network of Family History Centers, at major libraries (usually for local ports), and online.

If you take the microfilm approach, you'll have to make an educated guess as to which port was your ancestors' destination since most are organized by a combination of port and date. A good first guess is New York, so you may find the free Web site for Castle Garden (www.castlegarden .org), Ellis Island's predecessor, helpful. Some eight million are said to have arrived at Castle Garden between 1855 and 1890, but this database covers 1820–1892 and includes approximately 12 million records. Results are index-only, but if you find your ancestors here, you'll have the information you need to snag a copy of the manifest through NARA or other resources without having to search through multiple rolls of microfilm.

As with so many other topics, Joe Beine has done an excellent job of summarizing numerous indexes for various ports and post-1820 time periods (www.germanroots.com/passengers.html), and as with pre-1820 arrivals, Ancestry.com's immigration collection is the most inclusive resource online and offers the considerable bonus of being able to search all ports at once.

1891–1957

Starting in 1891, responsibility for the processing of immigrant arrivals shifted to a newly established superintendent of immigration. This organization evolved over time through a series of titles including the Bureau of Immigration, Immigration and Naturalization Service (INS), and as it's known presently, U.S. Citizenship and Immigration Services (USCIS).

While the inspections introduced during this period might have meant more scrutiny and anxiety for our ancestors, this transition marked the beginning of a positive trend for genealogists—the gradual collection of more information. By 1907, most records included all details mentioned previously plus marital status, last place of residence in the old country, birthplace, the name and address of the closest relative in the old country, final destination in the United States (usually including the name and address of a relative or friend), whether the traveler was able to read and write, who paid for the journey, how much money the person had (which we tend to find oddly fascinating), race, personal description, and state of health. If you're trying to retrace your ancestors' steps, this is the next best thing to a map.

A number of our ancestors were detained for health or other reasons, and these are often noted at the end of the ship's manifest for a particular trip. One notation you might see is "LPC," short for "likely to become a public charge." This was fairly common for young women traveling solo with no one to meet them, but could be applied to anyone

PG. S. S.	KAIS. AUG. VIC (Ham.Am.) *arrived* June 18, 1910

	Index No.	NAMES.	MANIFEST. Group. No.	No. Persons	CAUSE OF DETENTION.	
25f	30	Andriskiewicz, Antonio	5	1	LPC.	2.30
16m	31	Koch, Leib	26 16	1	"	2.15

Leib Koch, father of future New York City mayor Ed Koch, was detained at Ellis Island as LPC, "likely to become a public charge." *(courtesy of Ancestry.com)*

whom inspectors suspected might not be able to support himself. One of the more surprising examples I've tripped across is Leib Koch, father of the future mayor of New York City Ed Koch. Incidentally, Leib later went by Louis, a common example of an Americanization of a name made by the immigrant himself (and not by Ellis Island officials).

This period also ushered in Ellis Island, which opened on January 1, 1892, and continued to function until 1954. This processing station has become so inextricably linked in our minds with immigration that many of us assume our ancestors entered the country through Ellis Island whether they actually did or not. Of course, due to sheer volume, it's a logical starting place for those who aren't sure where their ancestors arrived. Assorted numbers are tossed about, but 12 million people are said to have alighted at Ellis Island and it's estimated that 40 percent of Americans have at least one ancestor (and probably more) among these millions.

The Ellis Island database available at www.ellisisland.org purports to include approximately 22 million entries for passengers and crew members arriving between 1892 and 1924, the height of Ellis Island's activity. That might sound counterintuitive. How could there be 22 million entries for 1892–1924 if only 12 million people arrived from 1892 to 1954? While it's conceivable that there's some gentle inflation involved, this inconsistency actually highlights an underappreciated reality—the fact that some of our ancestors disembarked at Ellis Island several times. Part of this is attributable to crew members who appear multiple times in the records since they naturally made many trips across the ocean. Another contributing factor is the "birds of passage" phenomenon. Many of our ancestors didn't intend to stay in the United States permanently. Rather, they planned to work here, make some money, and go home to spend the rest of their days as the richest fellow in the village. Even some who decided to stay in America made at least one trip home to bring back an old country bride. These repeat migrants are referred to as birds of passage. The well-known Cuomo family of New York is a classic example, with ancestors who went back and forth to Italy as many as four times before settling here.

In spite of the well-deserved attention that Ellis Island gets, it's important to be aware that plenty of other ports were active during this time. If you don't find your relatives immigrating through New York, you'll want to check others. Usually, the place they settled will provide a hint of where to look next. If they lived in Massachusetts, for instance, Boston might make sense, whereas those who lived in the South might have arrived through New Orleans, Charleston, or another southern harbor city.

Many of our ancestors also entered the United States by land through Canada or Mexico, a possibility that can be investigated using border crossing records. Partly because fares to Canada were less expensive, many detoured their way into America, and Mexican crossing records feature a startling parade of nationalities. Regardless of whether your ancestors were Russian, Syrian, French, or Japanese, you might just find them entering the country through Texas or California.

No matter when or where you think your ancestors might have arrived, you may wish to consult *They Came in Ships*, a much-beloved classic in the genealogical world. This slender volume by John P. Colletta provides a concise overview of the availability of passenger arrival records. Those who prefer to get their information online will find plenty to explore at www.genesearch.com/ports.html. Both of these resources include information on Canadian and Mexican border crossings.

Like records from earlier time periods, these can be found at the National Archives, through the Family History Library, selectively at major libraries, and online. In terms of what's available online, Ancestry .com's immigration collection offers the best one-stop shopping since it includes records for Ellis Island, an impressive array of other ports, border crossings, and so forth. One search here could bubble up your ancestor even if he entered the country through a port you never would have considered. Those of us with Ellis Island ancestors can also search the database at www.ellisisland.org through the Web site itself or indirectly through SteveMorse.org or pilot.FamilySearch.org. You may recall from Web site descriptions in chapter 2 that these last two will link you to records housed on the Ellis Island site itself, but make it easier to unearth those hard-to-find ancestors.

NATURALIZATION RECORDS

Perhaps I'm a fan of naturalization records because of my own. Naturalization is the process by which an alien becomes a citizen. As an army brat, I was born overseas to American parents and bounced into this world a dual national, so my parents decided to clarify the situation. The result is my naturalization file, which profiles what I suspect is the most proportionate "new" citizen on record: I was thirty-six months old, thirty-six inches tall, and weighed thirty-six pounds!

In my case, naturalization was something of a formality, but for your immigrant ancestors, it was one of the most memorable events of their lives. The paper trail created by this procedure also happens to be one of the best sources for revealing the name of the town your ancestors called home before coming to America.

Naturalization records parallel passenger arrival records in that more recent naturalizations are both easier to find and more detailed. Aside from the oaths of allegiance noted previously, you'll find few naturalizations for the colonial period since most immigrants then were considered to be British subjects. From 1790 to 1906, the naturalization process was usually handled through local courthouses and generated three rounds of paperwork:

- Declaration of intent—The immigrant declares his intent to become a U.S. citizen and renounces his allegiance to any foreign entity; typically includes name, country of birth, date, and signature (or "X" mark, if illiterate); also referred to as "first papers."
- Petition for naturalization—After a designated waiting period (usually two to five years), the immigrant petitions the court for formal citizenship; also referred to as "final papers."
- Certificate of naturalization—Issued to the immigrant once the petition is granted.

Records at some courts included more information than outlined above, so you might get lucky and learn more than anticipated, but the challenge in many cases is determining the correct court. While the accepted rule of thumb is to start with the county where your ancestor lived, your ancestor may have begun the process in one location, moved, and completed it elsewhere. Some lived in large cities where there were several courts, and even those in rural areas could confuse us by going through the process in another county. Why? Convenience. If he lived at the edge of a county fifty miles from the county seat, and the neighboring county's seat was only thirty miles away, guess which one he chose? That's why it's a good idea to put yourself in your ancestor's shoes by consulting a map and asking yourself what you would do. There's a decent chance he made the same decision.

September 26, 1906, is a milestone for naturalizations because this is the date they came under federal control. After this point, your ancestor still followed the same three-step procedure and probably went to the closest courthouse, but now standardized forms were used and his records were forwarded to the federal government. Genealogically, this is great news because these new forms required much more information, such as date and place of birth, port and date of entry, name of ship, and names of his spouse and children. In many cases, birth details for the spouse are also included, so you may be able to identify hometowns for two ancestors with a single document. This is especially important since women were automatically naturalized if married to a U.S. citizen (naturalized or not), so they rarely filed their own papers until laws changed in 1922 (a similar situation applies to children under the age of twenty-one at the time of their father's naturalization).

The benefit of the centralization of records that began in late 1906 is the fact that naturalizations after this date can be obtained through U.S. Citizenship and Immigration Services (go to www.uscis.gov, select "service and benefits" from the top menu, and click on "genealogy") even if you don't know the courthouse involved. A fifty-year privacy restriction applies, so check the Web site for details, but millions of us with ancestors who came as part of the massive Ellis Island era can access their records through a single source. At present, USCIS processing times to fulfill a request are running about four months, but if you're in a rush and think you know the relevant courthouse, you also have the option of trying to obtain records from the court because many retain a duplicate set of these records.

Because of their dispersion, naturalization records predating September 1906 can take more effort to locate, but your ancestor's local courthouse is the logical place to start. It's also worth checking the National Archives, especially for those living in major cities. The Family History Library has some of the naturalization records found at NARA and selected courthouses, so a few minutes checking the library catalog at FamilySearch.org may be time well spent. If the FHL has naturalization records for the county you're interested in, read the microfilm descriptions closely before ordering as some courts filed declarations and petitions separately, so obtaining copies of both documents may involve more than one roll of microfilm. Certificates were given to the freshly minted citizens and tend to have been passed down through the family, but in some cases, they may be found at the court (for instance, when people didn't return to the court to retrieve the certificate if it wasn't ready at the time of the naturalization), so it pays to be thorough.

If you'd like to learn more about naturalization records, *They Became Americans: Finding Naturalization Records and Ethnic Origins* by Loretto D. Szucs is highly recommended. Yet again, Joe Beine provides a well-organized set of links to direct you to what's available on the Internet (www.germanroots.com/naturalization.html), and though naturalization records are relative newcomers in the online world, Ancestry's immigration collection and Footnote.com both offer small but growing collections.

ANCESTRY.COM'S IMMIGRATION & EMIGRATION RECORDS COLLECTION

Throughout this chapter, you've seen repeated references to this collection (go to Ancestry.com, click the "Search" tab at the top, and select "Immigration & Emigration"), and for good reason. Available to subscribers and free at many libraries, this compilation of immigration-related databases is by far the most wide-ranging and comprehensive. In fact, it's estimated that 85 percent of Americans have ancestors in it. With well over 100 million records—many of them including digitized images of the original documents—there's a good chance that several of your immigrant ancestors are in here just waiting to be found by you.

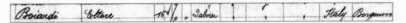

Ettore Boiardi, the future Chef Boyardee, arrived at Ellis Island in 1914 at age
sixteen. To test your search skills, you might want to see how many other com-
ings and goings of his you can find in this collection. *(courtesy of Ancestry.com)*

All Ellis Island arrivals from 1892 to 1954 are included, as well as
records for more than one hundred ports! Here's just a taste of what's
available:

- Philadelphia Passenger Lists, 1800–1945
- Border Crossings: From Mexico to U.S., 1903–1957
- Galveston Passenger Lists, 1896–1948
- Great Migration Begins: Immigrants to New England,
  1620–1633
- Wisconsin Crew Lists, 1925–1969
- Utah Pioneers, 1847–1850
- Boston Arrivals of Jewish Immigrants from Hebrew
  Immigrant Aid Society Records, 1882–1929
- San Francisco Chinese Exclusion List

One of my favorite hidden gems is the New York Emigrant Savings
Bank (1850–1883). You might wonder why a bank's records are included,
but if you're past thirty, you probably remember all the personal information you once had to supply your bank to open an account. Fortunately, this was true for some of our ancestors as well. This database is
particularly useful for those with Irish immigrant ancestors who lived
in New York City and the surrounding area, but you'll find Scots, Germans, and others—and not just ones from New York. If you're especially fortunate, your ancestor's record will furnish extra details. An
entry for a fellow named Patrick Grady, for instance, tells us his job and
employer and that he was born in 1823 in Youghal, County Cork, Ireland. It goes on to reveal that he's single, his father Thomas is deceased,

his mother Bridget Keefe is living in Ireland, and his sister Catherine Brennan is living in Yonkers. Quite a find!

An emerging area of focus for this collection is naturalization records. The first specific database that many turn to is U.S. Naturalization Records—Original Documents (1795–1972), but it's worth exploring to see what else is available, such as:

- Philadelphia, 1789–1880 Naturalization Records
- New York Southern District, World War II Military Naturalization Index, 1941–1946
- Minnesota Naturalization Records Index, 1854–1957

Another popular record set included in this collection is U.S. Passport Applications (1795–1925). While the Department of State has issued passports since 1789, they were not required until 1941 (with two brief exceptions associated with wartime security concerns: 1861–1862 and 1918–1921), so many Americans didn't obtain them. Even so, well

Family name	Given name or names
Boiardi	Ettore
Address	
1552 East 27th, Cleveland, Ohio	
Certificate no. (or vol. and page)	Title and location of court
1850934 -Vol.139,pg.32	U. S. Dist. Ct.,Cleve.
Country of birth or allegiance	When born (or age)
Italy	Oct. 22, 1897
Date and port of arrival in U. S.	Date of naturalization
May 10, 1914, New York	May 8, 1923
Names and addresses of witnesses	
Giacomo Favagrossa, 1636 Payne Ave.	
Thomas Coletto, 17440 Norwood Rd.,Lkwd.	

U. S. Department of Labor, Immigration and Naturalization Service. Form No. 1-IP. 14—3202

Index card for the naturalization of "Chef Boyardee." *(courtesy of Ancestry.com)*

over 1.5 million passports were issued between 1810 and 1925, and your ancestors' may be among them.

The odds of success in this collection improve if your ancestors lived more recently (over a million of the just-referenced passports were issued during 1912–1925 alone), were male (in the mid-1800s, 95 percent of passports were issued to men, but names of wives and children were often included), held certain occupations (e.g., diplomats, businessmen, members of the clergy, missionaries, and sea captains), were from a wealthy family known to travel for leisure, or were naturalized citizens (such individuals were more likely to secure a passport to protect themselves overseas and ensure their easy reentry to the United States). In another minor exception, aliens who had declared their intent to become citizens by filing first papers were eligible for passports in 1863–1866 and 1907–1920, so don't rule out the possibility of an application just because Grandpa wasn't naturalized yet when he returned to the old country to find a wife.

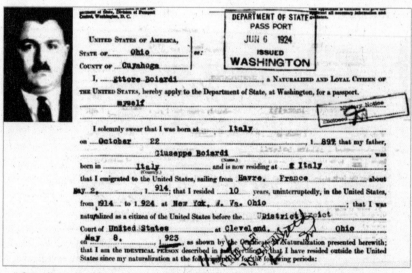

After obtaining citizenship in 1923, "Chef Boyardee" posed for a solemn photo and obtained a passport for a visit to Europe. *(courtesy of Ancestry.com)*

FOOTNOTE AND FAMILYSEARCH

Two other Web sites to bear in mind for immigration and naturalization records are Footnote.com and pilot.FamilySearch.org. At present, Footnote has some passport applications from 1795 to 1905, as well as naturalization records for varying time periods for Maryland, Massachusetts, Pennsylvania, southern California, and Cleveland, Ohio, and selected naturalization indexes for New York. While they can be searched free, viewing the documents requires a subscription.

The pilot version of FamilySearch.org currently makes it possible to search Ellis Island arrivals from 1892 to 1924 and will undoubtedly venture more deeply into immigration and naturalization records over time. This site is a perennial favorite among genealogists since it's free.

As seen from the Chef Boyardee illustrations, one of the advantages to accessing different Web sites is the fact that their collections are

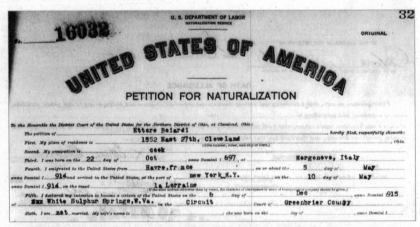

Chef Boyardee's petition for naturalization, found on Footnote.com, reveals that he declared his intent to become a citizen in Greenbrier County, West Virginia. *(courtesy of Footnote.com)*

complementary. While they frequently overlap, each one offers some unique content. In this case, Ancestry contains four passenger arrivals, a naturalization index, and a passport application for Ettore Boiardi. FamilySearch has two of his passenger arrivals and Footnote is the only one that includes actual naturalization records.

MORE IDEAS FOR FINDING THE HOMETOWN

Let's say you've done your homework and have a particular immigrant in mind. You have his name, and using census and other records, a country and rough year of birth—and maybe even an approximate year of immigration. But you still haven't been able to find out *where* in Belgium, Japan, or Russia he was born. You're still not out of luck. What follows are a few more of my favorite resources and techniques for rooting out this all-important clue.

USCIS

I mentioned earlier that you can request copies of post-1906 naturalization records from U.S. Citizenship and Immigration Services, but they also offer other genealogical records that might include your ancestors even if they were never naturalized. For instance, USCIS has millions of visa and alien registration files. One of my great-grandfathers emigrated from Ukraine in 1913, but never got naturalized. During World War II, noncitizens were required to complete Alien Registration Forms, so I was able to obtain a copy of his through the mail. Visit www.uscis.gov to learn more about what's available. Incidentally, in 2009 a decision was made to begin transferring some so-called A-files (Alien Files) from USCIS to the National Archives, so look for easier access to some of these records in the not-too-distant future.

Vital, Military, and Social Security Records

Several of the resources we've discussed in previous chapters might prove useful. Vital records such as marriage licenses and death certificates frequently include place of birth. While they often just give the country, you're sometimes rewarded with the town or region, so they're always worth checking.

Military records also merit a look. In my experience, World War I and II draft registration cards, Civil War pension files, and the U.S. Army Register of Enlistments (1798–1914) are among the most likely to include the hoped-for detail.

Finally, if you happen to have any immigrant ancestors who were working in America in the late 1930s or later, there's a good chance that their Social Security applications will reveal the place of birth. Better yet, that information will have been provided directly by the immigrant.

Newspapers, Religious Records, and Tombstones

We'll explore all of these resources in the next chapter, but I'll alert you in advance that they might just include your ancestor's hometown. Newspaper articles, especially obituaries, can be jammed with valuable information, including the place of birth for an immigrant. Luckily, their availability online has exploded over the last few years, with more emerging all the time.

Religious records offer another possibility. Perhaps the church or synagogue your ancestor attended will hold the missing piece of your puzzle. Check for marriage or burial records for the immigrant and baptisms for the children of the immigrants.

And if genealogists had their way, it would be a requirement to put the deceased's place of birth on his or her tombstone. That's not usually the case, of course, but this was done frequently enough that it's worth a try for your own ancestors. In fact, it was a tombstone in Ohio that told me where to look for Barack Obama's ancestors in Ireland several years ago—information I still haven't found replicated in any other source (see chapter 8, "Sleuthing in Action," for the full story).

For Unusual Surnames

If you still can't identify the town that your ancestor came from and you happen to be blessed with a slightly unusual name (sorry, this won't work if you're a Schmidt, Murphy, or Koval), go to SteveMorse.org and select the Ellis Island Gold Form. Enter the surname of interest and choose the "sounds like" option. If you get too many hits, try again using the "is phonetically" alternative. Scan the results and see if a pattern emerges in terms of hometown. Many of us have names that originate in one town or region in the old country, so you may be able to narrow your geographic focus using this tactic even if you can't find your own ancestor.

You can also try piggybacking off of the efforts of other researchers. To do this, click on the Family Trees tab at Ancestry.com, enter a surname, and select the relevant country. Just as with SteveMorse.org, look for any patterns in terms of birthplaces, but also be alert for any overlaps with your own tree. By doing this, I recently tripped across a distant cousin who had managed to snag an English marriage record for a shared Irish-born ancestor. He had lived in England for only a couple of years before reemigrating to America, but that was long enough to leave behind a trace that my newfound cousin had spotted, and I was the beneficiary of her research.

OLD COUNTRY RESEARCH

Once you discover exactly where your immigrant ancestor was born, you're prepared to tap into your old country past. Research overseas is very country-specific, so it's regrettably beyond the scope of this book, but I'd like to share enough to at least get you started. Your primary options for pursuing this research are:

- Using online databases for that country or region
- Accessing records available through FamilySearch and the Family History Library
- Continuing your quest in that country by either traveling there or hiring a researcher

While I completely understand the urge to jump on a plane and muck about in foreign archives, you probably won't be surprised to hear that you'd be better off starting with online databases and the FHL.

Records for a number of countries are available on two of the same Web sites that have featured prominently in this chapter, Ancestry.com and pilot.FamilySearch.org. Ancestry offers an international subscription that's presently heavy on British Commonwealth countries, especially the United Kingdom, Canada, Australia, and New Zealand, but also includes records for Germany, Italy, Sweden, France, and China (if you understand Chinese, check out www.jiapu.cn). FamilySearch's coverage is more global and more random. Both Web sites will undoubtedly continue to expand their international collections.

Among the first databases you should consult are emigration and arrival records for other countries. Some of these, such as Hamburg Passenger Lists (1850–1934) and U.K. Incoming Passenger Lists (1878–1960), are part of Ancestry's international collection, while others, such as Passenger Lists Leaving U.K. (1890–1960), are found on other Web sites like Findmypast.com.

In addition to the many journey-related databases, you'll want to investigate other records that may include your ancestors before their departure. Census and civil registration records for England, Scotland,

and Wales, for instance, are available from several sources. If a country's coverage is comprehensive enough, it might be possible to spot your ancestor in his hometown even if you were unable to find his departure or arrival records. This approach is not generally recommended because it's too easy to claim the wrong John McKaig (or whatever your ancestor's name was) if you didn't already know his hometown. But if you come up completely empty on your immigration research or just can't resist the temptation to play with old country records early on, you might get lucky, especially if your immigrants sported unusual names.

Depending on your heritage, you may find plenty of records to explore online. In fact, you might even be able to push back several generations without going any farther than your computer. I'm always jealous, for instance, of those with Swedish or Scottish roots (visit www.genline.com and www.scotlandspeople.gov.uk to see why), but a growing number of Web sites are offering more and more genealogical records online. It's a long Web address, but the International Genealogy Sleuth™ links at www.progenealogists.com/genealogysleuthi .htm allow you to browse many links by country or region, and you'll find even more at the volunteer-driven WorldGenWeb project (www .worldgenweb.org).

I'll just give you a heads-up that many European Web sites favor a credits or units system where you pay per record or for small batches of records, as opposed to subscriptions. This would be fine, except that some are not as search-friendly as they could be so it's not difficult to accidentally wind up paying for records for someone whose profile is similar to your ancestor's. Many allow you to narrow your search by time period or location, though, so the more you know before you venture in, the better prepared you'll be to pluck out your ancestor's record on the first try.

Regardless of your heritage, you should also make it a habit to explore pilot.FamilySearch.org and the FamilySearch library catalog.

The 2.4 million rolls of microfilm housed in Utah are so extensive that it's a rare family indeed that fails to make an appearance in them. But it's important to know that the point of entry for most of these records is by place, rather than by name. Most of the traces your ancestors left will not yet have been indexed by name, which is one of the reasons it's essential to learn exactly where they came from.

To find your ancestor, you'll want to search the library catalog for the place they lived, and for every administrative level that might apply. Just as we have towns, counties, and states, many countries have multiple territorial levels and some records are filed only one way. Perhaps local church records will pop up only if you search for the village, but census records will be found only if you search for the old country's equivalent of county. Once you identify your ancestor's hometown, spend a few minutes Googling your way to these other relevant place names and keep them handy for your searches.

To give you an example of how far-reaching these records are, I'll turn to a portion of my own family. Four of my great-grandparents came from villages that are located in present-day Slovakia, Poland, and Ukraine. All came from small villages, some with populations as low as a few hundred even today, and yet all four are found in FHL records. Coverage varies from everything I could possibly dream of for one Slovak village to twenty years of church records for one Ukrainian village, but all of them are in there and have been added to over time.

While the majority of these records would currently have to be ordered on microfilm or researched in Salt Lake City by you or a hired professional, that will gradually change. FamilySearch is digitizing and uploading records at a remarkable pace, so those Norwegian vital records you so badly want might be available only on microfilm now but will suddenly emerge online eighteen months from now. For this reason, it makes sense to poke around FamilySearch every few months to see what's new.

BON VOYAGE!

Crossing the pond to the hometown of your immigrant ancestor can be one of the more challenging stages in your research, but I hope that one or more of the ideas provided here proves to be just what you needed to help you make that leap. If so, please be sure to send me a postcard when you go visit your ancestral homeland!

7

THE BEST OF THE REST

There are so many genealogical gems out there that it's simply not possible to squeeze all of them into the pages of a single book. What follows is an attempt to acquaint you with some of the best resources available aside from census, vital, military, and immigration records.

Part of the fun of genealogy is the fact that there are so many records and repositories. Family historians are like the proverbial kids in a candy store every time a previously undiscovered or tucked-away collection of old papers emerges. But especially in the early stages of your research, it can feel a little overwhelming. So many to choose from . . . Where do you start?

The resources discussed here are the ones you'll want to turn to sooner, rather than later. Court records and newspapers, for instance, are both terrific for bringing your ancestors to life. They help you get past the "just the facts, ma'am" world of names, dates, and places and reveal your ancestors as real people with accomplishments, attitudes, and agendas. Though it's not strictly a "record type," DNA testing is included here because it opens a whole new realm of possibilities in terms of solving your personal history mysteries. And for good measure, I've tossed in a little help for figuring what the heck "fifth cousin twice removed" means. Read on to learn about these and a few other tried-and-true favorites.

RELIGIOUS RECORDS

Regardless of what your own beliefs may be, chances are that your ancestors belonged to a church or synagogue, and that religion played a central role in their lives. That's fortunate because their participation in the milestone rituals of their religions (such as marriage ceremonies) often left a paper trail. In fact, that trail may well predate the existence of vital records wherever they lived, which is why religious records so often supplement or essentially substitute for birth, marriage, and death records.

To find religious records, you'll naturally need to determine the religion of your ancestors. For many of us, that will be the same as what we adhere to today, but don't assume that's the case. Look for clues in your family records (e.g., Bibles, funeral or mass cards, etc.), obituaries (which often mention where the funeral is being held), and other documents you've obtained (I've often backdoored into a person's religion by Googling the name of the officiant listed on a government-issued marriage record). The cemeteries they're buried in (many older ones were associated with a particular church) and photos (such as a wedding party in front of a church) might also provide hints. But be open-minded: ancestors living on the frontier, for example, might not have lived close enough to a church of their own religion, so they may surprise you by showing up in records for a different denomination (at least until the

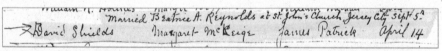

This notation for the baptism of my grandfather in the records of St. Peter's Roman Catholic Church in Jersey City, New Jersey, included a remark about his marriage. That was lucky for me because my grandparents married at a church that neither of their families regularly attended, so I might not otherwise have found their marriage record. Found on FHL film 1403372. *(courtesy of the author)*

population grew to the point where it could support a church of their usual faith).

As with vital records, religious records are highly dispersed, so locating them can be a bit of a challenge. If the house of worship your ancestors attended is still in place and serving the community, writing a letter is usually the best approach. You'll want to be very precise in your request, saying that you'd like a copy or complete transcript of your grandfather's baptism, because many churches use generic, prefabricated forms to respond to such inquiries. These forms often don't provide spaces for all the details included in the original records, so if your great-grandparents' birthplaces are noted, for instance, they won't be sent unless you specifically ask for that information. It's also considered appropriate to enclose a small donation as a gesture of gratitude. Even so, they're under no obligation to reply, so prepare yourself for the possibility that your check could be cashed with no response forthcoming. That's the exception to the rule, but it does occasionally happen.

If the church or synagogue you seek is just a memory, you can try contacting others of the same religion in the area and asking where local records may have been moved or consolidated. By way of example, it's not unusual for several former Catholic parishes to have been combined into one. You can also do a little homework to track down a headquarters or archives. Take a few minutes to look over the religion category on Cyndi's List (www.cyndislist.com/religion.htm) for a running start.

It's also a smart idea to make it a habit to check the library catalog of the Family History Library. To do this, go to FamilySearch .org, select the catalog, and use the "place" field for your search. Then review any hits for church records for that location. While the results are patchy, the FHL has been filming religious records around the world for so long that you can be sure that at least a couple of the communities your ancestors once called home will be among them.

Osturna, Slovakia—the ancestral home to every Smolenyak who's ever walked the planet—has one Greek Catholic church, and the FHL has its records back to the 1700s. If the FHL has records for Osturna, it's a good bet that at least some of your New England, Georgia, or Minnesota ancestors are in there as well.

NEWSPAPERS

Newspapers are a tremendous resource and offer jackpot potential. Most genies have a near obsession with obituaries since they're often loaded with detail, but this is just one of the possibilities. For any given ancestor, you might be able to spot birth and marriage announcements, graduations, moves, visits from others, military service, and so much more—and that's for ancestors with no measure of fame. If any notables adorn your family tree, you're probably in for an embarrassment of riches. You might even trip across an unexpected discovery—perhaps an account of Great-Grandpa's moonshine operation or the murder in the family that had been conveniently forgotten.

Until recently, though, newspapers were comparatively difficult to incorporate into your research. It's true that identifying the relevant newspapers, figuring out where they were housed, traveling to the appropriate repository, and then searching through countless issues hoping for a mention of your family might turn up a few family history gems, but then again, it might not.

Working with newspapers historically involved a calculation—would the outcome justify the time and effort spent? But over the last few years, technology has significantly altered this equation. Millions of pages have been digitized, made searchable, and uploaded to the Internet—and even tracking down the many newspapers that have yet to be digitized has become easier.

A good starting point is Ancestry.com's Newspaper & Periodicals

Collection, featuring a wide variety of publications from across the country and even overseas, but other possibilities include GenealogyBank .com (see chapter 2 for more) and NewspaperARCHIVE.com. All of these subscription-based sites provide access to multiple newspapers with wide geographic and time coverage. Whether you're looking for an article about a colonial ancestor from New England or an obituary about a second cousin who passed away last year, these collections might give you near-instant results.

ProQuest Historical Newspapers, available through many libraries, is another option. This collection focuses on the major newspapers such as the *New York Times, Washington Post, Chicago Tribune, Boston Globe*, and *Atlanta Constitution*. Most of us have at least a few ancestors who spent some time in metropolitan areas, so this is a particularly useful collection. If you prefer to surf from home, you can access this same content directly from the Web sites of individual newspapers. For instance, those interested in the *New York Times* can go to www .nytimes.com and search there. The archives portion of these newspaper sites tends to be slightly hard to find, so try using your browser's "find" feature to look for "archives," or try a regular query and look for an "advanced search" option to appear with the results. A modest fee usually applies, although at least a portion of the *New York Times* collection is free.

Still more alternatives are the Chronicling America site from the Library of Congress (http://chroniclingamerica.loc.gov) and Google's News Archives (http://news.google.com/archivesearch). The former is a growing collection of digitized newspapers from across the country focused on the 1880–1922 time period. It's somewhat random as each state makes its own decision about what to include, but over time, this free resource will become increasingly valuable for genealogists. This same Web site also includes a finding tool for ascertaining which repositories hold just about every American newspaper back to 1690. Google's News Archives is also random, but an effective means to search many online resources simultaneously. Finally, you may find the "Historical Newspapers and Indexes on the Internet" guide (www.researchguides .net/newspapers.htm) and OnlineNewspapers.com helpful in determining whether newspapers relevant to your research reside somewhere online.

COURT RECORDS

Say the word "court" and most of us immediately think of lawsuits and trials. While files from countless civil and criminal cases are indeed held in courts, that's just a fraction of what they offer to genealogists. The courthouse in the county where your ancestors once lived might turn up marriage registers, military discharges, naturalization files, adoption proceedings, guardianship papers, divorce records, and much more.

The court records that genies rely on most heavily, though, are those pertaining to property. We can't get enough of land and estate records! While these property trails are appreciated by all, those with deep American roots value them even more since they offer one of the best possibilities for learning about ancestors who lived during a time when other records were light on detail (e.g., census) or nonexistent (e.g., vital records in many areas).

Deeds include names of the seller (grantor) and buyer (grantee) as well as those of witnesses, and particularly in colonial times and rural areas, there's a good chance that at least some of the parties were related to one another. While the tendency is to think of houses and land, deeds were also used for other property—most notably, slaves. This is also true of estate-related documents such as wills, probate, and letters of administration. Names other than the deceased's are included and relationships are often spelled out. And though it may be distasteful, the harsh reality is that property records of all types are some of the most productive for researching ancestors who were once enslaved.

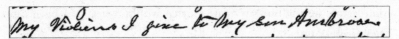

Just days before he died, blind musician James Finnegan of Lackawanna County, Pennsylvania, filed a will in which he left his violins to his soon-to-be-orphaned son, Ambrose. Because James died young, this document was key in proving his relationship to Ambrose. Ambrose grew up, married, and had a family that eventually included a grandson named Joe Biden, who would go on to become vice president of the United States.

Finding court records for your ancestors often entails a genealogical field trip. Some court records can be found online (try http://public records.netronline.com to see what might be available for the counties that interest you), but generally that's just the proverbial tip of the iceberg. Counties that put databases on the Internet typically have limited offerings (say, deed indexes for 1980 to the present), relatively few provide access to digitized records, and many have basic Web sites with no indexes or records at all. Still, it's worth inspecting these sites for basic information such as location and hours. They might also explain procedures for requesting copies by mail, or at least list phone numbers you can call for more details.

Another alternative is the Family History Library, which holds court records from across the country. Search the library catalog on FamilySearch.org for the relevant county, paying particular attention to listings found in the court records, land and property, and probate records categories. Once you do a little homework about what's available through the FHL and at the courthouse itself, you'll be in a better position to evaluate what the best approach for you might be.

While the choice is yours, I can't resist offering one piece of advice. If you had many ancestors who lived in a particular county for several generations, a road trip may be in order. You can obtain copies of many records long distance through the mail or perhaps by hiring a researcher in Salt Lake City, but there's no substitute for conducting research at the actual courthouse. That's how many genealogists have come across family history treasures that would never have been discovered otherwise.

But if you go, please be considerate of the employees who work there. Don't expect them to skip their lunch hour for you or listen to stories about your fascinating great-grandfather. It just takes a few demanding genealogists to wear out our welcome, so please think about the rest of us who may wish to research there one day. Should you opt for a field trip, I also suggest that you obtain a copy of *Courthouse Research for Family Historians* by Christine Rose to help map out a strategy to get the most from your trip.

CEMETERIES

Perhaps the easiest way to tell whether someone's a genealogist is to mention the word "cemetery" and watch the reaction. If he or she lights up like a Christmas tree, you're dealing with a genie. We love cemeteries because of the records they might hold, and, of course, for their tombstones. It may sound strange, but that weathered tombstone of a great-great-great-grandmother who died in 1834 may well be the closest physical connection you'll ever find to her. People pass away and houses get torn down, but tombstones—or at least, burial plots—often remain, so they're frequently the only place we can go to pay our respects.

While cemetery visits easily rate as high on the popularity scale as courthouse jaunts, there are considerably more virtual options for finding tombstones. Transcribing or taking digital photos of tombstones is one of the most widely spread acts of genealogical kindness, and there are quite a few online resources that might include a few of your ancestors. One of my favorites, findagrave.com, contains tens of millions of tombstone inscriptions and is discussed in chapter 2, but here are a few others:

- Interment.net—includes more than four million entries from more than five thousand cemeteries around the world

- JewishGen Online Worldwide Burial Registry (http://
  jewishgen.org/databases/cemetery)—more than half a
  million names of Jewish burials across the globe; available on JewishGen.org and Ancestry.com
- Nationwide Gravesite Locator (http://gravelocator.cem
  .va.gov)—from the Department of Veterans Affairs,
  searchable database of veterans and family members buried in government cemeteries, as well as those buried
  in private cemeteries since 1997 (data also available on
  Ancestry.com)

Local county resources such as genealogical or historical societies
might also hold such information, either online or perhaps in a book
available for purchase. You'll also find plenty of tombstones in the Photos & Map section of Ancestry.com, where you can search by name or
browse a variety of headstones by entering "tomb" or "grave" in the
keywords field. And if all this just whets your appetite to learn more,
consider spending a few minutes clicking your way around Joe Beine's
"Cemetery & Obituaries" research guide (http://www.researchguides
.net/cemeteries.htm) or add *Your Guide to Cemetery Research* by Sharon
DeBartolo Carmack to your library.

DNA TESTING

You've probably seen it on television and read about it in the newspapers, and it makes you think twice. More and more people seem to be
turning to DNA to peek into their past, but you can't help but wonder:
Just what is "genetic genealogy" and is there anything you could learn
from such testing?

The ABCs of DNA

Simply put, genetic genealogy is DNA testing that's done specifically for the purpose of learning about one's heritage. It's a complement to traditional genealogy, rather than a substitute, and the two play very well together. Using DNA to explore your roots is akin to using the Internet in that it will often help you go further faster. It can tell you about your deep ancestry (as in thousands of years deep), and in some instances, reveal something that the paper trail never could.

Genetic genealogy has been around for about a decade now, and the good news is that it's completely painless. No needles involved (though you should be prepared for a little cheek-swabbing). But is it really worth it? After all, the most popular tests run about seventy-nine dollars and up. Only you can decide, but if any of the following apply, you should probably at least consider adding DNA to your genealogical arsenal:

- You'd like to learn if others with the same surname share a common ancestor with you.
- You have a situation where the paper trail is iffy or has run out.
- You have a personal history mystery, especially one of those whispered tales of uncertain parentage (e.g., was Granddad's father really the wealthy banker your great-grandmother worked for before she married?).
- You want to save time, money, and effort in future research.

As you would expect with any technology, new types of testing continue to emerge, but there are two that have been available since the beginning and remain the favorite of genealogists: Y-DNA and mtDNA.

Y-DNA

Y-DNA testing uses the Y chromosome, which is sported only by males of the species. This has contributed to a myth that women can't play. Yes, we can. We just have to talk a male relative into taking the actual test on our behalf. Just as many take their first steps in genealogy by Googling their surname, most venture into genetic genealogy by testing their surname—and I was no different. So when I wanted to test the family I was born into, I picked up the phone and asked my father to take the test. If he had refused, I could have turned to one of my brothers or a paternal uncle or cousin.

The reason Y-DNA is so irresistible to family historians is that it's passed intact from father to son down through the generations. This is wildly convenient since surnames are passed the same way in most cultures. Barring a nonpaternity event (yes, they do happen, so make sure you can live with the results if they surface as a surprise in your family tree), the surname and Y-DNA travel through time in tandem— meaning that every man walking the planet today carries the same Y-DNA genetic signature as his father, grandfather, great-grandfather, etc. He's a living representative of those who came before, so, no—and this is yet another popular myth—it's not necessary to dig up the dearly departed.

Most of genetic genealogy boils down to a matchmaking game, and Y-DNA is no exception. Since it's still cost-prohibitive to test our entire genetic makeup, these tests rely on selected markers, which can be thought of as landmarks in the landscape of our DNA. Genealogists have piggybacked off the efforts of population geneticists who have identified markers that are highly variable—ones that are useful for distinguishing between peoples and even individuals. Your results will be presented as a number for each one of these markers, and it's these numbers (representing how often certain genetic patterns repeat themselves) that are used for finding matches.

When you use a conventional genealogy database and enter "John Smith," the system looks for matches for each letter: J-o-h-n. . . . This is exactly what happens with genetic genealogy, only numbers are used as the basis of comparison. Fortunately, all commercial testing companies have databases that automatically generate a list of matches for you. Provided you signed a release, you can then communicate with your genetic mates. Assuming that you've joined one of the thousands of surname studies that already exist (try Googling "genealogy DNA surname" to see if there's a project for your name), you'll want to look for matches among your fellow participants. If you want to extend the search still further, you can enter your results in free, public access databases such as www.ybase.org and www.ysearch.org to look for matches.

So what does a match mean? It means you share a common ancestor with that person. This kind of testing can't tell you that your most recent common ancestor is your mutual great-great-grandfather, but you know for sure that your lines converge at some point. In most surname studies, clusters of genetic mates emerge, and these folks become your research pals. If you're especially lucky, you'll find yourself in a cluster with others who have already done a lot more homework than you. I recently persuaded a man named Jim Shields to join the Shields project of which I'm a member, and he matched another participant perfectly. The other fellow had researched the family for twenty-seven years and knew exactly where Jim fit in, so Jim suddenly had 450 new relatives! And while I can't say this is an everyday experience quite yet, the databases are finally achieving critical mass—that is, there are now enough of us getting tested that this kind of outcome will become increasingly common.

If you are contemplating a Y-DNA test, I would suggest that you select at least a mid-resolution test—a test with more than thirty markers. Resolution in this case means much the same as it does with printers. The higher the resolution, the clearer the result—and low-resolution tests can sometimes lead to a misleading outcome. Fortunately, prices have come down enough that cost isn't the determining factor that it once was.

Mitochondrial DNA (mtDNA)

After tiptoeing into the world of genetic genealogy with a Y-DNA test, many become curious to see what else they can learn, so they move on to mitochondrial DNA. Many think of mtDNA as the maternal version of Y-DNA, and while there are certain parallels, it's important to understand the differences—starting with the mode of transmission. MtDNA is passed from mothers to both their sons and daughters, but the sons don't pass it on. This is fortunate because it means all of us—male and female—can take this test ourselves. As with Y-DNA, our test represents those who came before us, only in our maternal line—our mother, mother's mother, mother's mother's mother, etc.

But at this point, mtDNA is not quite as genealogically useful as Y-DNA. This is because it's largely been considered more of a deep ancestry test. If you're familiar with Dr. Bryan Sykes's best-selling book *The Seven Daughters of Eve,* you're aware that the basic premise is that 95 percent of those of European origin can trace their maternal roots to one of seven women who lived between 10,000 and 45,000 years ago. When you take an mtDNA test, you're learning which one of these "daughters of Eve" you descend from (it's estimated that there are thirty-some-odd on a global basis), and most companies will provide a color map showing roughly how and when your branch of the world's maternal family tree (referred to as your haplogroup) migrated out of Africa.

That's wonderful to know from an intellectual curiosity standpoint, but it usually doesn't tell you much about your recent roots. My maternal Irish forebears, for instance, have passed the H haplogroup down to me. H happens to be the most common in Europe (apparently H's maternal descendants were the most successful in reproducing, so roughly 30 to 40 percent of Europeans are also H), so I have literally millions of maternal cousins.

Fortunately, however, recent research has revealed that there's greater variety in mtDNA genetic signatures (called haplotypes) than previously thought, and this suggests that it will be of greater genealogical value than we had imagined. Also, a few companies have recently introduced full-sequence mtDNA tests, so in the not-too-distant future, the matchmaking game for mtDNA will become almost as effective as it is with Y-DNA.

MtDNA also has a role in dealing with specific genealogical conundrums. For instance, if your great-grandfather had fifteen children by three wives, and you can't quite assign all the children to the correct mothers, you might be able to test direct line maternal descendants of a few of the daughters involved and work your way back to their respective mothers. It takes a little strategizing, but it's possible. And finally, mtDNA is the tool that scientists most frequently rely on for history mystery situations, such as the Romanovs.

To Learn More About DNA

As the coauthor (with Ann Turner, M.D.) of *Trace Your Roots with DNA*, I can't hide the fact that I'm a longtime proponent of genetic genealogy, but if it's new territory to you, I encourage you to learn more before jumping in. Meander around the Web site of the International Society of Genetic Genealogy (www.ISOGG.org) and download the free guide on The Genetic Genealogist's blog (www.thegeneticgenealogist .com). Investigate the sites of the more popular testing companies (you might want to start with DNA.Ancestry.com, FamilyTreeDNA.com, and DNAHeritage.com) and consider looking into the latest kind of testing, which combines ancestral and medical results at companies like 23andMe.com. Incidentally, if you're curious about why my name is Smolenyak Smolenyak, you might want to watch the *Did She Marry Her Cousin?* video (on www.honoringourancestors.com) to see how I used Y-DNA to answer that question.

SORTING OUT RELATIONSHIPS

It's going to happen to you sooner or later. You'll trip across a distant cousin on the Internet and tie yourself in knots trying to figure out how you're related. Are you fourth cousins once removed, or maybe fifth cousins twice removed? What is all that "nth" stuff and just what does "removed" mean anyway?

The good news is that genealogy software calculates this for you. Depending on which package you're using, you've got a relationship calculator, kinship report, or something similar. Typically, you select the people you're trying to connect, run the tool, and—poof!—the answer is magically given to you.

Still, not truly understanding this tends to drive us nuts, so let's see if I can shed some light. The relationship between two people is expressed as "*nth* cousins *x* times removed," and the first step is identifying the common ancestor. Let's call him John Q. Ancestor or JQA for short. Once you've done that, count the number of generations that separate the JQA from Cousin A and then do the same for Cousin B (hint: it helps to sketch out a chart or use your software to do this). When you do this, don't count the generation you're in or the generation JQA is in; just count the intervening generations.

The lower of the two

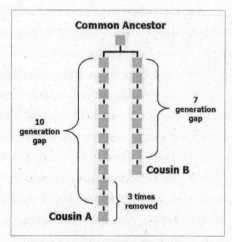

Cousins A and B are seventh cousins three times removed. *(courtesy of the author)*

generation gaps is the *n* in the phrase. If there are ten generations between JQA and Cousin A, and seven generations between JQA and Cousin B, then *n* = 7. Cousins A and B are seventh cousins of some sort.

Now take the difference between those same generation gaps; in this case, 10 – 7 = 3. In this case, Cousin A is three generations further *removed* from JQA than Cousin B is. This means that Cousins A and B are seventh cousins *three times removed*.

If both cousins are an equal distance from the common ancestor—say, seven generations—then they are seventh cousins, period. There's no "removed" involved when the cousins are in the same generation.

Because our brains all operate differently and this is a much-discussed topic among genealogists, I'd like to share a few links to tools, charts, and explanations of this same topic. One of them is bound to fit well with your style of thinking, whatever it might be.

- Interactive kinship calculator from Mark Tucker of ThinkGenealogy: http://www.thinkgenealogy.com/2009/07/25/interactive-kinship-calculator/
- Genealogy relationship chart from Kimberly Powell of About.com Genealogy: http://genealogy.about.com/library/nrelationshipchart.htm
- Steve Morse's tool for calculating relationships: http://stevemorse.org/relation/calculator.html
- Ancestor Search's cousin relationship calculator: http://www.searchforancestors.com/utility/cousincalculator.html
- Dick Eastman's explanation along with ideas from a number of his readers: http://blog.eogn.com/eastmans_online_genealogy/2009/07/what-is-second-cousin-once-removed.html

SHIFTING GEARS

The deeper you delve into genealogy, the more wonderful resources you'll discover. Before long, you'll probably find yourself adding maps, city directories, voter registrations, and much more to your bag of tricks. As much as I'd like to linger and cover them all, this book would never end if I did. Now that I've loaded you up with records, Web sites, and research tactics, it seems a good time to see how they all interplay in real life—and that's exactly what we'll do in the next chapter.

8

SLEUTHING IN ACTION

Over the last handful of chapters, we've been exploring a variety of records that genealogists use extensively. But anyone who's been researching their roots for a while will tell you that the true magic happens when you stir together the clues you've found from all these diverse sources. Perhaps a name found in a vital record, a date found in a census record, and a location found in a military record all combine to reveal your immigrant ancestor. It plays out differently each time, but weaving together the scattered snippets of information you discover to solve a family history mystery means you're truly becoming a roots detective.

To demonstrate the process of unraveling genealogical riddles, I thought it might help to share a couple of the adventures I've had the opportunity to pursue. I hope you'll find some inspiration along the way, and perhaps a few ideas, resources, or tactics to borrow.

THE QUEST FOR OBAMA'S IRISH ROOTS

Just before St. Patrick's Day in 2007, a press release went out announcing that then–presidential candidate Barack Obama was part Irish. In fact, on his mother's side, his Irish third great-grandfather, Fulmoth Kearney, is his most recent connection with any "old country" ancestry. When Fulmoth arrived in New York in 1850, all of Obama's other maternal ancestors were already here.

I was quoted in the press release, and as I have an unusual name, it's not difficult to locate me—and that's exactly what a number of Irish journalists did. The general gist of all the inquiries I received? So he's part Irish, but where in Ireland did his ancestors come from?

Bragging Rights

Being half-Irish myself, I wasn't very surprised by this interest in the specifics. I was aware that Dunganstown, County Wexford, was delirious when "native son" John F. Kennedy was elected president in 1960. His great-grandfather had emigrated to America, so Kennedy's political ascension gave Dunganstown bragging rights that it continues to exercise today. As recently as 1999, the former Kennedy household was converted into a museum. Likewise, his Fitzgerald heritage gave the village of Bruff in County Limerick something to boast about—especially when the Fitzgerald family Bible was used for his presidential oath of office.

Coupling Ireland's proclivity for claiming its prominent descendants with the obsession with Obama's roots (has any other political figure ever been so frequently obligated to remark on his family tree?), it was inevitable that my phone would start ringing. I both welcomed and dreaded the phone calls. Why? I like a challenge, but those of you with Irish heritage probably know how difficult it can be to identify places of origin in Ireland. Frankly, I wasn't sure I would succeed, but it was worth a try.

Finding Fulmoth

Obama's maternal roots are what I regard as typically presidential in the sense that they extend back deep—in most branches for centuries—in

America. Because of this, the preliminary research I had done proved to be straightforward. I relied heavily on U.S. Federal Census records to methodically march back generation by generation on his mother's side of the family tree.

As I did so, I scanned for any evidence of foreign births, and made my first such find in the 1870 census for one of his great-great-grandmothers, Mary Ann Kearney. Her father was from Ireland. He was listed as Falmoth or Fulmoth (a little hard to make out) and thirty-eight years of age. His name would turn out to be the proverbial mixed blessing. As my research progressed, I would find him as Fulmoth, Fulmouth, Falmouth, Fulmuth, Falmuth, and so forth—a bit of a nuisance though not unexpected. Kearney offered its own complications with spellings such as Kerney and Carney. But ultimately, it was worth the hassle because his name was distinctive and made him comparatively easy to pluck out. On balance, I was grateful to be dealing with a Fulmoth Kearney, rather than a John Murphy.

The Fulmoth Trail

With his unusual name, it wasn't difficult to locate his arrival record in the United States on Ancestry.com. Experimenting with various versions of Fulmoth and Kearney, I found him as Falmouth Carney (indexed as Falmouth Cainey). He had arrived on the *Marmion* in New York on March 20, 1850.

While most arrival records from this time period furnish just the basics, this one gave Falmouth's destination as Ohio, so it made sense when he showed up several months later in the 1850 census residing in Wayne Township, Fayette County, Ohio. I noticed others in the same

Falmouth Carney 1850 passenger arrival record. *(courtesy of Ancestry.com)*

household named Carney, Cleary, and Canada. No relationships were provided, but the Clearys would resurface later in my research.

By 1860, he had a family of his own and appeared in Deerfield, Ross County, Ohio, with his wife, Charlotte, and several children. A little digging at the Family History Library in Salt Lake City popped up his 1852 marriage to Charlotte Holloway in Fayette County, and I couldn't help but notice that the name of the justice of the peace was William Kearney—the same name as the head of household in Fulmoth's first home in America.

Around 1866, Fulmoth moved from Ohio to Jefferson Township, Tipton County, Indiana. This is where I had first spotted him in the 1870 census when I searched earlier for his daughter, Mary Ann. By the time of the 1880 census, he had passed away, so the documents I had gathered to this point briefly outlined Fulmoth's life in America—but now I needed to cross the pond. Fortunately, these same documents provided me with vital clues for doing just that.

Connecting the Dots

I mentioned earlier that one of the most effective techniques for research is what I refer to as "surround and conquer"—also known as collateral research. When you can't find what you're looking for by focusing on the paper trail of a particular individual, it's a good idea to broaden your search to include the trail of others associated with him or her, especially relatives.

In Fulmoth's case, I accidentally did this without even trying, simply by finding his arrival record. I was fortunate that such an early record showed the intended destination of the travelers, and more fortunate still that Fulmoth—and only two others, William and Margaret Cleary—were headed to Ohio. Typical for the time, most of their fellow passengers were heading for New York, but this troika stood out. Why were these famine-era immigrants going to Ohio? I didn't know, but I was glad of it—and even happier when I realized that William and Margaret were also in the same household with Fulmoth in the August 1850 census. Clearly, there was a connection.

I decided to focus on William and Margaret Cleary and easily found them in the 1860 census in Deerfield, Ohio, living with an older couple named Joseph and "Pharb Kearny" (Phebe Kearney). Hmmm . . . maybe Margaret Cleary was Ful-

Could Joseph and Pharb Kearny be Falmouth's parents? *(courtesy of Ancestry.com).*

moth's married sister and Joseph and Phebe were his parents. That would certainly explain why he had named his first daughter Phebe. It would also be a serious bonus as I hadn't expected to find his parents in America.

Fulmoth's Family

Using this notion as my hypothesis, I looked for records pertaining to all the people in this emerging family tree and started piecing it together. Unbeknownst to Margaret, the alleged sister, her future second husband was living next door in the 1860 census. By the time of the 1870 census, her older first husband had passed away and she had married Jacob Rohrer, the neighbor's farmhand. Her father had also passed away, but her mother Phebe was still living with her.

Through a combination of searching online records and Googling assorted names and locations, I continued to cobble together a likely family for Fulmoth—parents Joseph and Phebe, sisters Margaret and Mary/Mary Ann, and a brother named William. Particularly helpful was a family history Web site by a researcher named Roger Kearney. This site was tantalizing in that it included mentions of what appeared to be pockets of this same family—but Fulmoth was nowhere to be

seen. Still, I badly wanted to believe my blossoming theory because
Roger's site included a tombstone transcription for Fulmoth's possible
father that gave his birthplace in Ireland. In the hope that there might
be more clues, I commissioned an Ohio-based genealogist to go to the
cemetery and photograph all the graves. Roger had transcribed most of
them, but I needed to see photos of the actual tombstones myself.

In the meantime, I continued to mine his site for clues and that's
when I spotted another interesting transcription—the will of a Francis Kearney, dated January 28, 1848. In it, he left land owned in Ross
County, Ohio, to his brother, Joseph, "if he comes to this country."
Could that have been the spark for the departure of Fulmoth's family
from Ireland? I had assumed it was the famine, but could it have been
that Francis was Fulmoth's uncle and that his promise of land had lured
the family to America? According to Roger's site, the Kearney family
had been chain migrating to the United States since the late 1700s. If
my theory was correct, Fulmoth's branch would have been about the
last to leave the old country.

Francis Kearney leaves land in Ohio to his brother Joseph, but only if he comes
to America. Found on microfilm 288397 at the Family History Library.

Coming to America

I decided to see if immigration records could support a will-triggered migration and quickly found the evidence I was seeking. Fulmoth's probable father, Joseph, had arrived in New York on April 25, 1849, on a ship called *Caroline Read*.

As I had discovered earlier, Fulmoth, his sister and brother-in-law had followed in March of 1850. His likely mother, Phebe, arrived in New York on August 28, 1851, on a ship called *Clarissa Courier* with her children, Mary and William, and a forty-year-old woman named Catherine.

Yes, this all meshed nicely. Francis Kearney had died only a week after making his will in 1848. Allowing time for his brother back in Ireland to get the word and make appropriate arrangements, the family had left for Ohio in annual waves in 1849, 1850, and 1851 with Fulmoth riding the middle one.

Better yet, when the tombstone photos arrived from Ohio, it was possible to piece together still more of the puzzle. Parents Joseph and Phebe had died in 1861 and 1876 respectively. I already had an idea of what had become of Margaret, but the stones revealed that brother William had died in 1855, just a few years after arriving in America, and sister Mary Ann in 1866. Fulmoth and Margaret were the only ones in the family missing from the cemetery.

Previously researched census records showed that Fulmoth had named his children Phebe, Elizabeth, Martha, William, Joseph, Fulmoth, Mary Ann, Margaret, and Francis, and now I could see why. Martha was the name of his wife's mother and I can't explain Elizabeth, but the other seven names were those of Fulmoth's parents, siblings, and the uncle who had bequeathed the land that brought his family to America in the first place.

Joseph Kearney's tombstone pointed the way to Moneygall. *(courtesy of the author)*

To Ireland!

Thanks to the cemetery photos, I finally had the information I had hoped to find—the place of origin in Ireland. The tombstones for Fulmoth's father Joseph and brother William both indicated that they were born in Moneygall in Kings County (now County Offaly). The time-worn inscription above reads: "Sacred to the memory of Joseph Kearney Sen., born in Moneygall, Kings County, Ireland, Died October 30, 1861, aged 67 years." Who'd have thought that the key to solving the mystery of President Obama's Irish roots would be a couple of tombstones in Wayne Township, Ohio?

Although I was confident about Moneygall, the logical last step was to locate the family in records over in Ireland. To this end, I enlisted the help of Irish expert Kyle Betit of ProGenealogists.com. There were a number of possible parishes to consider and Murphy's Law kicked into high gear as Kyle tried parish after parish without success. The family was nowhere to be found. Largely through a process of elimination, he gradually zeroed in on the diocese of Limerick and Killaloe and made contact with the Anglican priest there. But Murphy wasn't quite done with us.

The vicar was friendly, but none too swift in responding. As he later admitted, "I get a lot of these requests and it was only after the nature of the possible link with Senator Obama was revealed that I fully engaged with the search." Based on the information gathered from the earlier research, we provided him with a list of names and estimated dates for the baptisms of Fulmoth and his siblings and the marriage of his parents. Fortunately, an index had been prepared for the Templeharry Rectory of the Church of Ireland about twenty years earlier, so he was able to cross-reference our wish list with the index and find most of the requested records, which he gamely took digital photos of and e-mailed. Now we had substantiation from both sides of the ocean that the family hailed from Moneygall.

They're Celebrating in Moneygall

So Moneygall gets the bragging rights and they're not wasting any time in celebrating. There's talk of a heritage center, and if you search YouTube, you can find the popular song "There's No One as Irish as Barack O'Bama." Just be forewarned—it's one of those tunes that gets stuck in your brain.

FINDING (THE REAL) ANNIE MOORE OF ELLIS ISLAND

On January 1, 1892, an Irish teenager named Annie Moore tripped down a gangplank and into the pages of history, but just briefly. As the first arrival at Ellis Island, she became an instant celebrity splashed on the front page of all the newspapers, but almost as quickly, vanished into the obscurity that greeted most of her fellow immigrants.

Fast forward a century and Annie suddenly became a celebrity again. Against the backdrop of the refurbishment of Ellis Island, her tale was unearthed and she reemerged as the poster child for the American immigrant experience, and a symbol of the Irish diaspora. Hers was a glamorous, go-west-young-woman saga (she was said to have migrated in stages all the way to Clovis, New Mexico) sprinkled with a captivating mix of pioneering spirit and tragedy.

Too bad it wasn't true.

I discovered that this oft-recounted tale of Ellis Island's first arrival was wrong while working on a documentary about immigration about half a dozen years ago. As a national symbol of two countries, Annie's statue stands at both Ellis Island and its Irish counterpart in Cobh, Ireland, so tracking down her descendants to appear in the film seemed an obvious thing to do. It also proved to be easy because there were plenty of newspaper articles about her family members.

Historical documentaries tend to be visually challenging since the selection of images is usually limited. It's not as if everyone was running around with cameras and camcorders

Annie and her brothers at the Cobh Heritage Center in Cork, Ireland. *(courtesy of the author)*

a century ago. Because of this, I decided to track down some of Annie's paper trail to complement her story, but quickly ran into trouble. I found one census record, then another, then her marriage record and other documents—and all of them indicated a birthplace of Illinois, not Ireland. Clearly, this was the wrong Annie.

It baffled me how we could get her story—and our history—so wrong so fast. As I tried to unravel what had happened, I discovered that several decades ago an elderly woman had told her family that her mother—who truly was named Annie Moore—was the Annie Moore whose story was then resurfacing as a result of the restoration of Ellis Island. We tend not to second-guess the great-aunt Mildreds in our lives, so her family accepted the story at face value. When she passed away, one of her relatives happened to see a documentary about Ellis Island, and called those involved to tell of his family's connection to Annie. In this way, the family—and the story of *their* Annie—managed to slip into the cracks of American history. It was as much timing as anything since we were freshly curious about Annie, and no one troubled to sub-stantiate the story. After all, it would be a peculiar claim for another family to make, wouldn't it?

Some years later, I made my accidental discovery. There wasn't enough time to track down the true Annie for the project I was work-ing on, but she became a bit of an obsession for me because I felt she deserved to have her story known. Like a detective, I struggled to sniff out her trail, but the task was daunting and questions arose from the very day Annie landed. Her arrival records stated that she had traveled on the S.S. *Nevada* with younger brothers named Anthony and Philip, but newspaper accounts of the day provided confusing and conflicting reports of alleged siblings named Tom, Joe, Anthony, and Philip. And the *New York Times* reported that Annie's parents were named Matt and Mary, but there was no such family to be found in other records. Her name didn't help either. Looking for an Annie Moore in the 1890s was a classic needle-in-a-haystack scenario. So many shared her name and I had no clue what had become of her. Did she leave New York? Did she marry into another surname? Did she die young?

Frustrated after several years of my stop-and-go quest—and even more motivated after seeing a photo of the wrong Annie in the Amer-ican National Tree exhibit at the National Constitution Center in Philadelphia—I made an impulsive decision. I had begun blogging several months earlier, and came up with the idea of blogging a con-test offering a thousand-dollar reward for the first proof of what had become of the true Annie Moore. My fellow roots-sleuths responded enthusiastically by chipping in research, records, and theories, nudging us along a convoluted path of clues that taunted us by stubbornly refusing to reveal the finish line.

In retrospect, the first solid move forward was a posting by a researcher named Tracy Stancil. Tracy remarked that vital records indexes included an Anthony Moore who died in 1902 at the age of twenty-four—just about right to have been Annie's brother of the same name. Others had also noticed this, but discounted it for various reasons, but since we were stalled, it seemed a good idea to obtain the record.

It was intriguing to see that Anthony's father was named Matthew. That's what the newspapers had said, and at the time, Matt Moore wasn't a common name. On the other hand, the certificate gave his mother's name as Julia, while we were expecting Mary. Still, we wondered if this could possibly be Annie's brother.

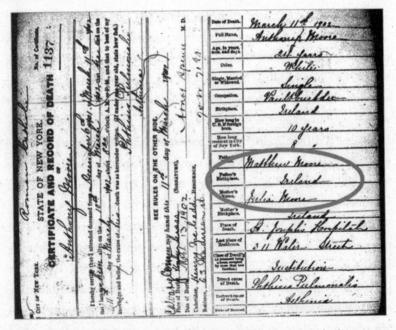

Death certificate of Anthony Moore, Annie's possible brother. Found on microfilm 1322709 at the Family History Library.

A possible 1900 census record for the family sent mixed signals. *(courtesy of Ancestry.com)*

Just about everyone had begun the search by looking at census records, but now we took another look to see if we could find a Moore family headed by a Matthew and Julia. Sure enough, there was one. But their appearance in the 1900 census sent a host of mixed messages. On the plus side, we knew this couple had a son named Anthony, and the census revealed a daughter named Annie of a likely age. Now we had a Moore family headed by Matt with children named Anthony and Annie. We also noticed that there was a daughter named Mary. Perhaps she had been there for Annie's arrival and the newspapers had confused her for the mother instead of a sister. But there was no Philip and the record indicated that Annie and her siblings had been born in New York—although it looked as if the birthplaces had been written in after the fact. At this point, we didn't know what to think. Was this Annie's family or not?

I realized that one of the best chances of determining whether this was the correct family was to look for a connection to Philip. If we could tie together all those names—Matt, Anthony, Annie, *and Philip* into one Moore family—that would be fairly convincing. So I focused on Philip and was well rewarded. Philip's 1920 federal census, 1915 New York State census, and World War I draft registration card all linked him to a mother named Julia. He wasn't with the family in the 1900 census (and the 1910 census was mysteriously absent as sometimes happens), but it was plain now that Philip also belonged to this family.

If there was any lingering doubt, though, the 1921 naturalization record for Philip—discovered by the New York City commissioner of records, who had also joined the hunt—erased it. The record stated that Philip had arrived on January 1, 1892, on the S.S. *Nevada,* just as we would have hoped. He was definitely Annie's brother. This was a giant step forward as we now had traction on Annie's family in America, but there was no sign of Annie herself and we were stranded in 1921.

Employing the "surround and conquer" tactic, I hoped that continuing to focus on Philip might somehow lead to Annie, so I looked for him in the 1930 census. And there he was with a wife, and better yet, a daughter named Anna. This was an exciting moment because it might well be possible to find this daughter who was born in the 1920s.

But obstacles appeared at every turn. More mucking about in vital records revealed that Philip had died in a car accident in the 1940s. Cemetery records led nowhere, so I tried to contact the funeral home that handled his burial, only to learn that its potentially valuable records had gone up in smoke when destroyed by a plane that fell out of the sky back in the 1960s. I then set my sights on his widow and child and managed to trace his widow to a town in New Jersey, but sadly, the last person who might have remembered something about her had passed away a couple of years earlier.

I knew it was a long shot, but at this point had nothing to lose, so I decided to look for the birth of Philip's daughter Anna in an index of New York City births. I knew I wouldn't be able to access the birth certificates themselves due to privacy restrictions, and the odds weren't good because Anna isn't exactly the most unusual of names. But I finally caught a break. There was only one Anna Moore registered in the time period I was estimating based on her age in the 1930 census.

I had no way of knowing whether this was the correct Anna, but I entered the name Anna and her birth date in the Social Security Death Index. Of course, I hoped she was alive, but had to investigate the possibility that she might not be. Eleven candidates were listed. None had died in New York City, but several had died in the state of New York, so I concentrated on them first, thinking they were the most promising.

Finally, the genealogical gods smiled on me. I picked the name that called to me the loudest and researched people associated with her. Dialing a fellow who was probably her son, I started explaining the purpose of my call: "Hi, you don't know me, but my name is Megan and I'm a genealogist. I'm researching a woman named Annie Moore who was the first immigrant through Ellis Island . . ."

That's as far as I got before Michael Shulman told me to stop—that I had the right family. I couldn't believe that I had called the right Anna's family on my first try! Still, this was only a partial victory because he was unable to provide information about Annie. He knew he was related to her, but didn't know the specifics of what had become of her.

We chatted for a while and the conversation meandered with Michael making a comment along the way about a "crazy aunt" who used to show up at the family weddings. Finally, he suggested that I speak with his sister Pat. I called her, but while she also knew of Annie, she struggled to recall more. At some point, I asked her about the crazy aunt her brother had mentioned and that proved to be the catalyst that opened up her memory banks (hint: if relatives can't remember something when you interview them, keep them talking). The now deceased aunt apparently made it a habit to remind folks of the family's tie to Annie. And that recollection caused Pat to blurt out the name Shyer. At least, that's what it sounded like. She said she thought that Annie had married a guy named Gus Shyer.

I was elated—and grateful that Pat had listened to her elders (I would later split the thousand-dollar prize between Pat and the commissioner of records for their contributions to the search). After our call, I hit the census databases looking for Annie Shyer. It took me a while, but I finally found an Annie married to Joseph Au*gus*tus Schayer—not exactly the first spelling that came to mind.

A search of New York City vital records indexes turned up what appeared to be her death in 1924, and when I received the certificate itself (death certificates being more open to the public), I finally knew for sure that I had the right Annie. Equipped with details from the certificate, my husband and I made a quick jaunt to New York and found ourselves standing over her unmarked grave in Calvary Cemetery in Queens, the anonymous resting place of perhaps the most celebrated immigrant in a nation of immigrants.

I played Sherlock a little longer to learn more about Annie's life and track down sixteen of her descendants to invite them to a family reunion in New York. They were now scattered in half a dozen states. Some knew of the link to Annie, while others had never heard of her. To my delight, most agreed to travel to New York, but when Sam Roberts wrote an article that appeared on the front page of the *New York Times,* the family reunion morphed into an international press conference.

Annie's life was tough. She lived in tenements, watched many of her children die before the age of three from poverty-related causes, and her family was too poor to afford a tombstone for a plot that sheltered eleven people. But I appreciated that her tale was much more representative of the immigrant struggle than the story that had been told. The happy

The empty patch of green is where Annie was buried with many of her children. *(courtesy of the author)*

ending we always hope for came from the success of her descendants. Just a few generations removed from the old country, they were living the proverbial American dream, thanks in part to Annie's sacrifices.

I was delighted when her descendants reciprocated, orchestrating a fund-raising initiative that culminated in a moving memorial dedication in late 2008. The ceremony featured Ronan Tynan singing "Isle of Hope, Isle of Tears," a song that tells part of Annie's story and still makes me well up every time I hear it. Thanks to her family and the efforts of a bunch of avid genies, Annie will never be forgotten again.

Annie's descendants found the perfect way to honor their no-longer-forgotten immigrant ancestor. *(courtesy of the author)*

9

PASS IT ON

True, you might be drawn to genealogy for the thrill of the hunt, but I've found that the common thread that unites all roots-seekers is a desire to connect. Family history helps you connect with your ancestors and living kin, even if they're fourth cousins once removed you've never met before.

So it would be a pity to keep all your discoveries to yourself—or worse yet, take them to your grave with you (not to be morbid here, but one day you'll *be* an ancestor). At least half the reason for tracing your roots is the joy of sharing.

This chapter will survey a variety of ways to protect, preserve, and share the results of your sleuthing. Family documentaries, scrapbooks, Web sites, donating your research to appropriate repositories, reunions—all of these are steps worth considering. But some less conventional approaches might appeal to you as well.

You'd be surprised how many ways there are to capture and disseminate aspects of your family history, and since we all have our own preferences, I want to give you a lot of food for thought. In fact, I hope you'll think of the following as a menu of ideas that you can pick and choose from according to your own tastes. *Bon appétit!*

FAMILY HISTORY BOOKS

Writing a family history book might sound daunting at first, but it doesn't have to be. Over the last few years, plenty of new resources have emerged to give you more options and help. Any genealogical software you purchase, for instance, will give you the ability to generate assorted reports of all the names, dates, and places you've entered. Select whatever appeals to you, intersperse some photos and brief narratives, and you've got at least a basic family history book to share with relatives. If you're slightly more ambitious, you can write and self-publish an actual book using a general publishing service like Lulu.com or a more specialized one such as familyhistorypublisher.com.

Those thinking of creating a book for a gift or keepsake (perhaps for your parents' golden wedding anniversary or an upcoming reunion) might want to look into MyCanvas (go to Ancestry.com and select the "publish" tab at the top). This allows you to design a number of eye-candy books or charts (I have a framed five-generation pedigree in my office) that you'll be proud to share. If you already have a family tree on Ancestry.com, all your data and documents will automatically be pulled in for you, and all you'll have to do is decide how you want it to look. Insert new pages, customize backgrounds, add embellishments, toss in more photos or family papers—in a sense, it's like virtual scrapbooking.

You might also want to consider books that capture one aspect of your family history. Gather up all those annual, state-of-the-family holiday missives you've written or received over the years and bind them, or make sure that Grandma's recipes get passed down to the next generation by collecting them and giving copies to everyone at the next get-together (do it yourself or with a company like heritagecookbook.com).

Getting creative with these mini-projects makes it more fun for you

Flat Stanley does time in the stocks in Colonial Williamsburg while researching his roots. *(courtesy of the author)*

and for your intended audience. I once had Flat Stanley (if you're not familiar with him, go to flatstanley.com or read about him on Wikipedia) do his roots for my nephew. Among other things, he went to Colonial Williamsburg, acquired a tricornered hat, and spent some time in the stocks—all to the amusement of my nephew and his classmates.

If all of this is more than you have time for, treat yourself to one of numerous guided or fill-in-the-blank books such as *A Grandparent's Legacy: Your Life Story in Your Own Words* or *The Mommy Journal: Letters to Your Child*. And finally, if you've got the wherewithal, you can commission an experienced family history writer to do the heavy lifting for you (check out www.warrencarmack.com (select "family history writing and editing") and www.turtlebunbury.com).

FAMILY DOCUMENTARIES

If writing isn't your thing, maybe you're a born producer. As with books, you can do this yourself and perhaps share with the rest of the world on YouTube or RootsTelevision.com (see the RootsTube option to upload) or tap into the expertise of others. If you'd rather hire someone else to interview the family matriarch or assemble a video family history, there are quite a few companies that specialize in this (www.familydocumentaries.com, www.lifetimereel.com, www.familylegacypro.com, www.bobxi.com, etc.) or you can search for just the right person at www.personalhistorians.org, the Web site of Association of Personal Historians (hint: some of them will write your family history too).

FAMILY REUNIONS

Ah, reunions! Those multipurpose events where you can reminisce with your favorite cousin, pay tribute to your ancestors, add the babies and toddlers to the family tree, let others know of your latest findings, create memories, get a couple of relatives to provide DNA samples in between their chili dogs and beer, and scout for likely prospects in the next generation to eventually pick up where you left off.

While I'm a big believer in reunions, I'm going to suggest that you prepare yourself by reading a few books, subscribing to *Reunions Magazine* (www.reunionsmag.com), and tapping into other resources such as www.familyreunions.com. I learned the hard way. Without giving it much thought, I planned my first reunion back in the 1990s and took forty Americans whose parents, grandparents, and great-grandparents had come from the same village over to Slovakia where we met our old country cousins. It was an amazing experience, but with the benefit of hindsight, I realize I should have practiced domestically first. So please do as I say and not as I did.

Reunions are terrific, not only for getting everyone together, but because they also create focus. All those projects you've been meaning to get to suddenly have a deadline since reunions are such a great opportunity to share them. I recall that one reunion lit a fire under me to gather and scan photos of 150 living relatives so I could arrive at the event with a massive family tree showing how we were all related (hint: kids are drawn to these charts if they've got faces in them). Another time, I mocked up a tabloid with actual family history for a reunion, and suspect far more read this colorful, abbreviated version than would have read an actual book. Another great reunion project? Time capsules. Companies such as Heritagetimecapsules.com furnish a range of products for this purpose.

This faux tabloid was a way to share family history in a fun and easy-to-digest format. *(courtesy of the author)*

REACH OUT VIRTUALLY

These days, there are many ways to connect with kin—both close and distant—online. Perhaps you're already a webcam-equipped grandparent or college student who stays in touch with the folks back home through Skype. Maybe like hundreds of other genealogists you'd like to share your research or your ancestor's journal entries through a blog (see the "personal research" and "documentary" categories here: http:// blogfinder.genealogue.com). Then there are the genies who practically live on Twitter, using its global reach to find strangers who share their last name and researchers in other countries, and the Facebook loyalists who post their genealogical discoveries along with snaps from yesterday's pool party.

All of these are effective ways to reach out to your scattered family members, but you also have genealogy-oriented alternatives such as those provided by MyFamily.com, Geni.com, and Genoom.com. When I decided to wean a village-focused association off the expensive, hard-copy newsletters I was mailing, I established a group on MyFamily .com. That was over a decade ago and hundreds of far-flung cousins still share photos, records, birthdays, and the latest news on a regular basis. All you have to do is decide what suits you. I suggest giving several of these options a test run, but if, like me, you happen to turn into a hybrid blogger-tweeter-Facebooker with additional Web sites, don't say I didn't warn you.

GET CRAFTY

If you're the creative sort, genealogy is a pastime that plays well with other hobbies. I've always been impressed with the ways people have found to combine their roots with painting, quilting, and other activities. Over the years, I've seen cross-stitched family trees, Christmas ornaments adorned with ancestors' faces, and an extraordinary array of family history scrapbooks. In fact, you can find quite a few books devoted specifically to heritage scrapbooks (or check out www.scrapbookmemoriestv.com).

Quilts have long been a mainstay in capturing not just family but community history. It's not unusual to come across an antique quilt with the names of all the members of a particular church or small town on the individual squares. Similarly, many quilters piece together panels representing their genealogy—perhaps their ancestors' names, family homesteads, and ships sailing across the ocean. If you'd like to see a sampling, just search online images for terms like "heritage quilt" and "memory quilt." Incidentally, if this appeals to you but you're not skilled in this area, there are companies that will do it for you, making quilts of just about anything, including cherished baby clothes, family photos, or all those T-shirts you've collected on your travels.

My husband and I encircled the top of our dining room with names of our ancestors. *(courtesy of the author)*

Being a noncrafty type, I've found other ways to incorporate my genealogy into my everyday life. In our dining room, which we've dubbed the hall of ancestors, my husband and I have a gallery of ancestors' photos, iconic Ellis Island images, and the names of some of our forebears wrapped around the top of the room (using burnished vinyl words ordered through www.wonderfulgraffiti.com). Whatever your preferences and talents, there's a fitting way to help your ancestors escape the confines of your genealogy software so they can be appreciated on a more regular basis.

PHOTO FORWARD

I confess that I feel sorry for our descendants who will have to deal with the countless digitized images we'll leave behind, but most of us today are dealing with the opposite problem. The majority of our ancestors left behind very few photos. It took me years to hunt down pictures of seven of my eight great-grandparents and I still have no idea what one looked like, so the photos I have are precious to me.

The obvious way to make sure that these photos outlive me is to digitize and distribute them. The originals are rare, and I've seen far too many sepia-toned faces staring back at me at estate sales and on eBay to assume that the worst won't happen. So my insurance is to scan and share them. I share them in online family trees, on Facebook, on CDs given out at reunions, in digital photo frames—any way I can. Next up, I plan on making virtual puzzles and e-mailing them to family members (http://puzzletouch.com). Incidentally, if you happen to come from one of those families that went into image-overdrive a couple of generations earlier than most, there are companies like ScanDigital.com that can digitize those boxes of photos, albums, slides, negatives, and even home movies for you. Ready, set, digitize!

BACKUP PLANS

A few years ago, my home got pummeled by Hurricane Isabel. Weather forecasters in the area exaggerated potential dangers with such regularity that the "boy who cried wolf" syndrome had kicked in. My husband and I didn't take the warnings seriously, so it wasn't until we saw an eighty-foot tree in our yard come crashing down that we realized we had to get to the basement—and pronto. What did I grab in those few moments before hunkering down? A hard drive with my family history.

We weathered the storm, but the experience made me think more seriously about putting safety nets in place for my genealogy. Having a portable hard drive was a good start, but now I have several in different locations. Selected photos, documents, and mementos now reside in a fireproof safe, and I've invested in archival supplies (see http://warletters.com/preserve.html for guidance and links to companies that sell these products) to help preserve my treasures.

Next on my list is to investigate companies like LegacyLocker.com (described as "the safe and secure way to pass on your online accounts" should something happen to you) and Arcalife.com, which offers a "time capsule" feature to "lock away files, comments and pictures and reveal them when the counter expires to an e-mail list of your choice." Coming soon on Arcalife will be a "beyond the grave" function that will allow you to record messages to be sent to loved ones in the future. At this point, I honestly don't know whether I'll sign up for any of these services, but their very existence is making me think about a backup plan for all my online accounts.

For that matter, it's prompting me to consider ways to ensure that the physical output of my research outlasts me. As much as I'd like to think that someone will be thrilled to receive several filing cabinets of research, I need to look into alternatives such as donating it to appropriate genealogical and historical libraries, societies, and archives (I plan on

browsing repositories here: www.uiweb.uidaho.edu/special-collections/
Other.Repositories.html) and including those arrangements in my will.
Perhaps the Family History Library and Library of Congress (www
.loc.gov/rr/genealogy/gifts.html) would accept copies of some prepared
materials. I know that I would be beyond thrilled to discover a family
history written by an ancestor during one of my genealogical jaunts, so
perhaps I can make that happen for some future relative.

GENETIC TRACES

Over half a million genealogists have already left genetic traces by taking DNA tests and sharing their results in assorted databases such as
ybase.org and ysearch.org. Those looking toward the future might also
wish to leave untested DNA samples for forthcoming generations. That
might sound a little odd, but I can't begin to fathom what might be
possible down the road, so it doesn't hurt to leave some DNA just in
case it could prove useful in some way. If this interests you, go online
and search the phrase "DNA banking" to explore your options.

I'll also admit that I plan on ordering DNA portraits for my husband
and myself (see www.dna11.com)—not so much to leave a trace, but
because I have a wall where side-by-side genetic profiles would be perfect.

THE BIGGER PICTURE

Yet another way to share snippets of your family history is to participate
in initiatives that extend beyond your relatives. For instance, you might
wish to add your immigrant ancestors' names to the Wall of Honor at
Ellis Island (www.wallofhonor.org). Or you can participate in online
memory projects such as the following:

- www.linkory.com—link your memories of certain events,
  dates, and rites of passage with others'

- www.ahamoment.com—share your aha moment with
  the world

One of my personal favorites is Andrew Carroll's initiative, The Legacy Project, to protect and preserve war letters (http://warletters.com/mission.html). Since it was launched a little over a decade ago, more than eighty thousand letters have been saved.

MEMORABLE FAREWELLS

There's been a trend in recent years toward customized tombstones, and while some lament them as tacky, most genealogists will tell you that they're all for anything that might give them a sense of their ancestors as people. A tombstone etched with the deceased's beloved tractor or shaped like a mailbox for a onetime postman? Makes perfect sense to most genies.

But this isn't the only funeral-related trend. Now we can have documentaries produced (see www.sentiment-farewells.co.uk and www.funeralrecording.com for examples), create an online memorial (Legacy.com), add a solar-powered video panel to a tombstone (Vidstone.com), keep our loved one close with "cremains jewelry," or skip all that and dedicate a tree (atreeinstead.com).

A SENSE OF PLACE

Not surprisingly, most of the ideas shared here have focused on people, but place plays an important role in our lives and memories as well. As it happens, there are plenty of ways to capture, preserve, and share the places that mean something to us. For instance, if your next family reunion is held in your ancestral hometown, why not familiarize attendees with your family's homes, schools, churches, and workplaces by arranging a place-based scavenger hunt (have them go in teams and take photos to prove they went to each location)? Want something more lasting? Have a painting or sketch of your home done by an artist like Dena McKee (www.denamckee.com/bio.html) or have your house history researched by a professional like Marian Pierre-Louis (http://field stonehistoricresearch.com/house.htm).

Maybe you'd rather share your memories virtually through online projects. Many such as the Maine Memory Network, Greater Cincinnati Memory Project, and Documenting Arkansas are state- or city-specific (search "digital memory projects" and state library and archive Web sites to find links), but you can also participate in broader ones like:

- Place + Memory (http://placeandmemory.org)—"If you could go back, where would you go?" Answer this question and your response might end up on NPR.
- Here Is Where (www.hereiswhere.org)—Let everyone know about forgotten historic spots across the United States.

Whatever your style and preferences, there's an appropriate way to record the places in your heart.

SOMETHING WORTH LEAVING BEHIND

Several years ago, singer Lee Ann Womack had a hit song called "Something Worth Leaving Behind." Part of the refrain from this song went, "I may not go down in history. I just want someone to remember me." I suspect that if we were all honest with ourselves, we'd admit that this resonates with us. It's only natural to hope that your life is meaningful not just to yourself, but to others, and that you'll be remembered when you're gone. And I think it's a reasonable assumption that our ancestors felt the same way.

Genealogy is a fun and meaningful way to honor our ancestors and possibly secure a little slice of posterity for ourselves in the process. I hope the ideas shared here—not just in this chapter, but in this entire book—have inspired you to give some thought to the legacy you inherited, as well as the one you'll pass on to future generations. If so, I promise that your descendants will appreciate it.

Best wishes with your ancestral quest!

Appendix

INTERVIEW GUIDES AND QUESTIONS

Ancestors (www.byub.org/ancestors/charts; select "research questions")

Capturing the Past (BYU) (www.byub.org/capturingpast)

Cyndi's List (www.cyndislist.com/oral.htm)

Family Tree Magazine (www.familytreemagazine.com/article/Oral-History-Interview-Question-Lists)

Hart, Cynthia, and Lisa Samson. *The Life Stories Workshop: How to Collect and Preserve the Oral Histories of Your Family and Friends.* New York: Workman Publishing Company, 2009.

StoryCorps Question Generator (www.storycorps.org/record-your-story/question-generator)

Szucs, Loretto Dennis, and Sandra Hargreaves Luebking. *The Source: A Guidebook to American Genealogy.* Provo, UT: Ancestry, 2006.

GENEALOGY SOFTWARE LINKS AND REVIEWS

About.com Genealogy (http://genealogy.about.com/od/software_mac/Genealogy_Software_Macintosh.htm)

Cyndi's List (www.cyndislist.com/software.htm)

GenSoft Reviews (www.gensoftreviews.com; includes Mac, iPhone applications, etc.)

Mac Genealogy Software Information (www.macgenealogy.org/mac -genealogy-software)

Genealogy Software

Ancestral Quest (www.ancquest.com)

Family Tree Maker (www.familytreemaker.com)

Legacy (www.legacyfamilytree.com)

Master Genealogist, The (TMG) (www.whollygenes.com)

Reunion (www.leisterpro.com; for Mac)

RootsMagic (www.rootsmagic.com)

ONLINE FAMILY TREE SERVICES

Ancestry.com

Geni.com

Genoom.com

MyHeritage.com

WeRelate.org

SOURCE CITATION HELP

About.com Genealogy (http://genealogy.about.com/od/citing/a/sources .htm)

Cyndi's List (www.cyndislist.com/citing.htm)

Mills, Elizabeth Shown. *Evidence Explained: Citing History Sources from Artifacts to Cyberspace* and *Quicksheet Citing Online Historical Resources*. Baltimore: Genealogical Publishing Co., 2007.

ProGenealogists (www.progenealogists.com/citationguide.htm)

Permissions and Acknowledgments

I would like to thank Alessandra Lusardi, Linda Konner, Julian Alexander, Anna Kirkwood, Claire Hungate, Alex Graham, Stephen Morrison, Anna Sternoff, Kate Griggs, Nancy Resnick, Tricia Conley, and Anya Roberts-Toney for performing miracles to bring this book to life. Everyone had to cope with impossible deadlines, particularly Anna Kirkwood, who gamely handled all the celebrity-related aspects of this book, and made it seem easy to the rest of us. I'd also like to thank my saintly husband, Brian Smolenyak, and talented sister, Stacy Neuberger, for gamely enduring yet another book-birthing season with me. I don't know how you put up with me, but I'm so grateful you do!

Special thanks to Ancestry.com, Arizona Department of Health Services, Joe Beine, Cook County Clerk's Office (Illinois), Chris Dunham, Footnote.com, the Family History Library, and GenealogyBank .com for generously providing permission for images used throughout the book.

Grateful acknowledgment is also made to the following for permission to reprint portions of previously published material:

"Crossing the Pond with Your Immigrant Ancestors," written by

Megan Smolenyak Smolenyak, included in materials sent to Ancestry
.com subscribers in April 2009.

"Genetic Genealogy: What Can It Offer?," written by Megan Smolenyak Smolenyak, published by BBC on www.bbc.co.uk.

"The Quest for Obama's Irish Roots," written by Megan Smolenyak
Smolenyak, published in the November/December 2008 issue of *Ancestry* magazine.

Who Do You Think You Are? is produced by Shed Media US/Wall to Wall Media in association with Is or Isn't Entertainment.

Executive Producers for Shed Media US
  Alex Graham
  Lucy Carter
  Jen O'Connell

Executive Producers for Is or Isn't Entertainment
  Lisa Kudrow
  Dan Bucantinsky
  Don Roos

Co-executive Producer
  Bryn Freedman

Consulting Producer
  Lee Metzger

Supervising Producer
  Anna Kirkwood

With special thanks to Anna Kirkwood for her contribution to this book as well as Alexandra Orton, Linda Ngov, and Bryan Cooper.

Who Do You Think You Are? is a trademark of Wall to Wall Media Ltd and is used under licence.

Visit www.nbc.com/who-do-you-think-you-are/